PRACTICE WHAT YOU TEACH

Many teachers enter the profession with a desire to "make a difference." But given who most teachers are, where they come from, and what pressure they feel to comply with existing school policies, how can they take up this charge? *Practice What You Teach* follows three different groups of educators to explore the challenges of developing and supporting teachers' sense of social justice and activism at various stages of their careers: White pre-service teachers typically enrolled in most teacher education programs, a group of new teachers attempting to integrate social justice into their teaching, and experienced educators who see their teaching and activism as inextricably linked. Teacher educator Bree Picower delves into each group's triumphs and challenges, providing strategies and suggestions for all teachers along with her in-depth analysis.

By understanding all these challenges, pre-service and in-service teachers, along with teacher educators, will be in a better position to develop the kind of political analysis that lays the foundation for teacher activism. This timely resource helps prepare and support all educators to stand up for equity and justice both inside and outside of the classroom and offers a more nuanced portrait of what the struggle to truly "make a difference" looks like.

Bree Picower is an Assistant Professor in the College of Education and Human Services at Montclair State University and Core Member of the New York Collective of Radical Educators (NYCoRE). She is the co-editor of the annual *Planning to Change the World: A planbook for social justice teachers* published by NYCoRE and the Education for Liberation Network.

The *Teaching/Learning Social Justice* Series
Edited by Lee Anne Bell
BARNARD COLLEGE, COLUMBIA UNIVERSITY

Critical Race Counterstories along the Chicana/Chicano Educational Pipeline
Tara J. Yosso

Understanding White Privilege: Creating Pathways to Authentic Relationships across Race
Frances E. Kendall

Elusive Justice: Wrestling with Difference and Educational Equity in Everyday Practice
Thea Renda Abu El-Haj

Revealing the Invisible: Confronting Passive Racism in Teacher Education
Sherry Marx

Telling Stories to Change the World: Global Voices on the Power of Narrative to Build Community and Make Social Justice Claims
Edited by Rickie Solinger, Madeline Fox, and Kayhan Irani

Educator Activists: Breaking Past Limits
Edited by Catherine Marshall and Amy L. Anderson

Interpreting National History: Race, Identity, and Pedagogy in Classrooms and Communities
Terrie Epstein

Social Justice, Peace, and Environmental Education Standards
Julie Andrzejewski, Marta P. Baltodano, and Linda Symcox

History as Art, Art as History: Contemporary Art and Social Studies Education
Dipti Desai, Jessica Hamlin, and Rachel Mattson

Storytelling for Social Justice: Connecting Narrative and the Arts in Antiracist Teaching
Lee Anne Bell

Promoting Diversity and Social Justice: Educating People from Privileged Groups, Second Edition
Diane J. Goodman

Actions Speak Louder than Words: Community Activism as Curriculum
Celia Oyler

Practice What You Teach: Social Justice Education in the Classroom and the Streets
Bree Picower

PRACTICE WHAT YOU TEACH

Social Justice Education in the Classroom and the Streets

Bree Picower

Routledge
Taylor & Francis Group

NEW YORK AND LONDON

First published 2012
by Routledge
711 Third Avenue, New York, NY 10017

Simultaneously published in the UK
by Routledge
2 Park Square, Milton Park, Abingdon, Oxon OX14 4RN

Routledge is an imprint of the Taylor & Francis Group, an informa business

Library of Congress Cataloging in Publication Data
Picower, Bree.
Practice what you teach : social justice education in the classroom and the
streets / Bree Picower.
p. cm. -- (The teaching/learning social justice series ; 13)
Includes bibliographical references and index.
1. Social justice--Study and teaching--United States. 2. Teachers--United
States--Political activity. I. Title.
LC192.2.P53 2012
370.11′5--dc23
2011047693

ISBN: 978-0-415-89538-5 (hbk)
ISBN: 978-0-415-89539-2 (pbk)
ISBN: 978-0-203-11825-2 (ebk)

Typeset in Bembo
by Taylor & Francis Books

Printed and bound in the United States of America on sustainably sourced
paper by IBT Global

Dedicated to past, present, and future members
of the New York Collective of Radical Educators

CONTENTS

SERIES EDITOR INTRODUCTION

The Teaching/Learning Social Justice Series explores issues of social justice—diversity, equality, democracy, and fairness—in classrooms and communities. "Teaching/learning" connotes the essential connections between theory and practice that books in this series seek to illuminate. Central are the stories and lived experiences of people who strive both to critically analyze and challenge oppressive relationships and institutions, and to imagine and create more just and inclusive alternatives. My hope is that the series will balance critical analysis with images of hope and possibility in ways that are accessible and inspiring to a broad range of educators and activists who believe in the potential for social change through education, and who seek stories and examples of practice, as well as honest discussion of the ever-present obstacles to dismantling oppressive ideas and institutions.

Lee Anne Bell, Series Editor

ACKNOWLEDGMENTS

As a scholar-activist who has been working as part of a collective for the last decade, I have been fortunate to have a family of passionate educators with whom to develop the ideas in this book. The understandings about teaching, organizing, and social justice that I write about have come out of the collective struggles and successes that we have worked on together. Over our countless meetings, retreats, protests, actions, film screenings, and study groups, we have put our heads together and wrestled with the current context of education and the role of teachers in the movement for social justice. For this I am grateful for the dedication of the core members of the New York Collective of Radical Educators, particularly: Keith Catone, Rita Kamani-Renedo, Ariana Mangual Figueroa, Edwin Mayorga, Seth Radar, Sam Coleman, Alanna Howe, Rosie Frascella, Natalia Ortiz, María del Carmen Ponciano, and Margrit Pittman-Polletta, and Karla Tobar.

In my role as a scholar-activist, my writing often falls behind the pressing needs of organizing and teaching. If it weren't for the invaluable support and ever-present genius of Dr. William Waters, this book would still be a seed that existed only in my mind. I am also indebted to Grace Ahn for her careful reads and uncanny ability to anticipate every next step. Thank you to my editors Catherine Bernard and Lee Anne Bell for their trust in my work.

Acknowledging the shoulders of the giants that have supported my growth as someone dedicated to teaching, I express my gratitude to two of the world's most powerful teachers that I have been so lucky to know and love: Carrie Secret and Suzanne Carothers. These two extraordinary women have guided my growth and given me the kind of detailed and longitudinal love and support that has changed the course of my life.

Just as teachers in this book have found allied peers in their struggles for justice, I am grateful to have found such a community of people with whom to participate in engaged scholarship. To my fabulous education academic family, I feel so lucky to have such incredible colleagues, friends and peers. Thank you for your dedication and friendship: Curtis Acosta, kahlil almustafa, Wayne Au, Patrick Camangian, Tony DeJesus, Jeff Duncan-Andrade, Maddy Fox, Rita Kohli, Kevin Kumashiro, John Lynch, Anne Marie Marshall, Leigh Patel, Madeline Perez, Rosa Rivera-McCutchen, Tammy Spencer, David Stovall, Danny Walsh and Susan Wilcox. Additionally, I'd like to acknowledge the senior scholars whose work, commitment, and personal support have been invaluable: Bill Ayers, Pedro Noguera, Jean Anyon, and the late Joe Kincheloe and Asa Hilliard. I'm also grateful to have found an academic home supportive of my work at Montclair State University thanks to Ada Beth Cutler, Tina Jacobowitz and the ECELE Department.

Over the past several years, one of the most exciting parts of my work has been the opportunity to work in coalition with the TAG network made up of national teacher activist groups and organizations. I am grateful to have been able to build relationships with these allies: Tara Mack at the Education for Liberation Network; Bill Bigelow and Jody Sokolower at Rethinking Schools; Pauline Lipman, Rico Gutstein, and Aisha El-Amin at Teachers for Social Justice Chicago; Karen Zapata and Jeremiah Jeffries at Teachers 4 Justice, San Francisco; Anissa Weinraub at TAG-Philly; Stephanie Schneider and Kathy Xiong at Educators Network for Social Justice Milwaukee; and the members of TAG-Boston.

I have had the pleasure of working with countless teachers whose energy and dedication is inspiring and I'd like to particularly acknowledge the members of the NYU Social Justice Critical Inquiry Project and NYCoRE's New Teacher Underground.

On a personal note, I'd like to especially acknowledge the undying support of my parents to which I am eternally grateful. I'd also like to recognize my extended family and friends: the Hochschuler clan, April and Samantha Freilich, Jamal Giles, Kristine Larsen, Liza Mostsinsker, Chris Powers and Anna Sop. Where would I be without all of you? Much love to all of you.

APPENDICES: FURTHER RESOURCES

Teacher Activist Groups

Teacher Activist Groups (TAG) – A national coalition of grassroots teacher organizing groups. Together, they engage in shared political education and relationship building in order to work for educational justice both nationally and in our local communities. The individual groups are listed below. http://www.teacheractivistgroups.org

Association of Raza Educators (Los Angeles) – An association that believes in community change through critical consciousness and democratic education. http://www.razaeducators.org/

Educators Network for Social Justice (Milwaukee) – A network of practicing educators promoting pro-justice curricula and policies so that all students in the Milwaukee area are better served. http://www.ensj.org

Metro Atlantans for Public Schools (Atlanta) – A network of progressive public school employees, parents, students and allies who believe that public education should be democratic, well-funded, and community supported. http://map school.wikispaces.com/

New York Collective of Radical Educators (NYCoRE) (New York City) A group of public school teachers and their allies who work for educational justice both inside and outside of the classroom. They create curriculum, organize teachers around a variety of issues and coordinate teacher led inquiry groups. http://www. nycore.org and http://www.facebook.com/NYCoRE

Teacher Action Group (Boston) – A group of Boston-area educators and allies that work together to organize around principles of social justice and education for liberation. TAG Boston is made up of K–12 teachers, former teachers, and other allies, and has drawn teachers from the greater Boston area. http://tagboston.org/

Teacher Action Group (Philadelphia) – An organization that seeks to strengthen teacher voices in schools and policy decisions. http://tagphilly.org/

Teachers for Social Justice (Chicago) – An organization that works to fight for social justice in Chicago and gets the voices of educators into the public discussion of school policies. http://www.teachersforjustice.org/

Teachers 4 Social Justice (San Francisco) – A grassroots, non-profit teacher support and development organization whose mission is to provide opportunities for self-transformation, leadership, and community building to educators in order to affect meaningful change in the classroom, school, community and society. http://www.t4sj.org/

National Social Justice Education Organizations and Teaching Resources

Education for Liberation Network – A national coalition of teachers, community activists, youth, researchers and parents who believe a good education should teach people—particularly low-income youth and youth of color—to understand and challenge the injustices their communities face. http://www.edliberation.org/

Gay, Lesbian and Straight Education Network (GLSEN) – An organization that strives to assure that each member of every school community is valued and respected regardless of sexual orientation or gender identity/expression. http://www.glsen.org

IndyKids – a free paper that aims to educate children on current news and world events from a progressive perspective and to inspire in children a passion for social justice and learning. It is geared toward kids in grades 4 to 8 in New York City. IndyKids is produced with the support of Indymedia New York City and individual donations. http://www.indykids.net

The People's Institute for Survival and Beyond – A national and international collective of anti-racist, multicultural community organizers and educators dedicated to building an effective movement for social transformation. http://www.pisab.org/

Planning to Change the World: A Plan Book for Social Justice Teachers – A planbook for educators who believe their students can and will change the world. It is designed to help teachers translate their vision of a just education into classroom activities. Co-edited by Education for Liberation Network and The New York Collective of Radical Educators. http://www.justiceplanbook.com

Rethinking Schools – A non-profit magazine and publishing house that focuses on teaching for social justice, anti-racist education, and issues of equity and equality in public education policy and practice today. They publish Rethinking Schools Magazine, various books and resources on teaching for social justice, and offer many resources online. www.rethinkingschools.org

Safe Schools Coalition – An organization that is working to make schools safe places for all children regardless of gender identity or sexual orientation. Their website contains a large collection of resource materials for educators. http://www.safeschoolscoalition.org

Teaching for Change – An organization that provides curriculum guides and other resources to help teachers engage students in innovative classroom activities that deal with issues of equity and social justice. They maintain a rich webstore with Busboys and Poets bookstore which is a one-stop shop for social justice education books and resources. http://www.teachingforchange.org

Teaching Tolerance – An organization dedicated to reducing prejudice, improving intergroup relations and supporting equitable school experiences for our nation's children. They provide free educational materials including a magazine and curricular kits to teachers and other school practitioners. http://www.tolerance.org

What Kids Can Do – An online publication that features young people's lives, learning, and work, and their partnerships with adults both in and out of school. http://www.wkcd.org

Zinn Education Project – An organization that promotes and supports teaching a people's history in middle and high school classrooms. To access the free teaching activities, visit the site and register at: http://www.zinnedproject.org/

1

TEACHER ACTIVISM

Social Justice Education as a Strategy for Change

If the United States hopes to maintain any semblance of a public education system, or a democracy for that matter, teacher activism is a critical necessity. The "public" nature of education is rapidly being stripped away by market-based reforms that are pushing an agenda of privatization. Slick marketing campaigns, round-the-clock news stories, and even full-fledged movies such as *Waiting for Superman* depict teachers as lazy and (with their greedy unions) as the cause of public school failure. By turning the hearts and minds of the general public against teachers (and their unions, their pensions, their seniority, etc.), politicians have succeeded in implementing mass teacher lay-offs, to the tune of 40,000 pink-slips nationally in 2010 (Epstein, 2010) and the deterioration of union benefits and bargaining rights in state after state across the country.

By conveniently glossing over the role that poverty, resource distribution, and institutional racism play in educational success, the current so-called "education reformers" are clearing the path for full-blown privatization of public education using the "bad teacher" as their rallying cry. With these fighting words surrounding the context of education, teachers must participate in the struggle to keep education public and to push for greater justice and democracy in the system. Just as we saw in the mobilization of the Occupy Wall Street movement, mass teacher mobilization is required to recalibrate the debate on what schools, students, and communities need.

Across the country, grassroots groups of teachers have emerged to create organizations such as the New York Collective of Radical Educators, Teachers for Social Justice in Chicago, and Teachers 4 Social Justice in San Francisco (Au *et al.*, 2005/2006; Doster, 2008), Teacher Action Group in Philadelphia, Educators Network for Social Justice in Milwaukee, and more. These groups have created a national Teacher Activist Group network (TAG) that is actively working to organize teachers, in coalition with parent, student, and community groups "to work for educational justice both nationally and in our local communities" (Network of Teacher Activist Groups, 2009). Such groups are rallying around a wide array of issues, such as the rise of market-based school reforms and privatization, the school-to-prison pipeline, nationwide educational budget cuts and lay-offs, the need for culturally relevant curriculum, and more. Teachers uniting and forming mass movements played a significant role in the Wisconsin union uprising of 2011 and has precedents in global struggles such as Oaxaca, Mexico (Denham, 2008). A social movement driven by teachers and teacher-unions is one of the few forces standing up to the attacks that public education is facing in the current context of the United States.

While more and more educators are joining such activist groups to struggle for educational justice, they are still just a small fraction of the teaching force. It is not an understatement to acknowledge that most of the 83% White and predominately middle-class teaching force (US Department of Education, 2008) are not ready to pick up protest signs to start marching in the streets as many of them do not acknowledge the political nature of education. In fact, as a teacher educator, when I ask my pre-service teacher education students why they want to be teachers, the overwhelming response is because they "just love kids." This lack of a broader analysis of the political nature of education points to a huge gap between who teachers currently are in the United States and the vision of teachers as activists fighting to intercede in social injustice.

As a scholar-activist and a teacher educator myself, I see my role as trying to narrow this gap. Working on multiple levels, my teaching and activism centers on preparing and supporting educators who will stand up for equity and justice both inside and outside of the classroom (New York Collective of Radical Educators, 2003). One of my main outlets for this work is as a core member of a grassroots teacher activist organization called the New York Collective of Radical Educators (NYCoRE). NYCoRE is a group of public school educators "who believe that education is an integral part of social change and that we must work both inside and outside the classroom because the struggle for justice does not end when the school bell rings" (New York Collective of Radical Educators, 2003). NYCoRE works with politically active teachers to respond to local and national educational policies by organizing protests, conferences, and study groups, and creating curriculum and resources for use in classrooms.

In my other role as a teacher educator, my goal has been to prepare teachers to enact the role of teacher activist. Most of my students, however, do not come to the profession predisposed to think about the roles that equity, diversity, and justice have to do with elementary school teaching. Like all teachers who start by meeting their students where they are, I have to engage my students to think about their often unexamined beliefs about who they are and where they come from, and how that impacts the way they see students who are different from themselves. I want my students to begin to question taken-for-granted assumptions about power, privilege, and various forms of oppression and how these impact education and the educational outcomes of their future students. Through my courses, students examine the ways in which they themselves were taught and in what ways this reinforced or transformed the inequalities that they are uncovering.

My students react in a variety of ways to my courses that explore these topics. Some, as one might imagine, react quite defensively and oppose the idea that topics such as race and homophobia have a place in their teacher preparation program. These students wholeheartedly hang on to mainstream ideologies about students of Color and urban communities, using many discursive tools that block a critical analysis of inequality, particularly around racism. Without this political analysis, the gap between their desire to maintain the status quo and the goal of teaching from a social justice perspective is unlikely to close. Much of my teaching centers around helping these students recognize that inequality in fact does exist, and that mechanisms such as racism, patriarchy, and neoliberalism maintain it. Fortunately, other students say that the course content is inspiring and they become highly motivated to develop curriculum from their emerging understandings of social justice.

It was quickly apparent that one or two semesters of critically oriented coursework was insufficient to support my graduates to become social justice educators. To address this, I started a Social Justice Critical Inquiry Project (CIP) with former students of mine who wanted support from this perspective in their first years of teaching. My initial thinking was that CIP could serve to "incubate" these teachers while they got their first year or two of teaching under their belts, and that by then they would be ready to join groups such as NYCoRE. Unfortunately this was not the case. While the CIP teachers did develop powerful curricular units on social justice topics such as racism, child labor, and gender roles to name a few, the teachers did not seem to move their work outside of their classrooms as activists.

Treating each of these groups of educators that I work with, 1) oppositional pre-service teachers, 2) emerging social justice educators, and 3) developed teacher activists as separate groups, I have done research with and written several articles about each distinct group over the last several years. As I started to explore why the CIP teachers were not developing into teacher activists in the way I had anticipated, I started to think more about the connections between each of these groups of teachers and what shapes the development of increasingly critical and active educators over time. This book is an attempt to look closely at this continuum from opposition to action, examining the obstacles and the pathways toward teacher activism, and the role that teacher education and professional development can play in expanding social justice education from the classroom to the streets.

Social Justice Education: What Is It?

In the last decade, the term and concept of "social justice" in education has both come into vogue and come under fire (Labaree, 2004; Stern, 2006). Rather than allowing this term to be abandoned or co-opted, it is critical for those of us who see education as a vehicle for liberation to be clear about what we mean when we say social justice education (SJE). SJE necessitates the ability for educators to engage on three levels. The first is for teachers to have a recognition and political analysis of injustice and how it operates to create and maintain oppression on multiple levels. The second is teachers' willingness and ability to integrate this analysis into academic teaching in the classrooms. The third is that teachers must have the mindsets and skillsets to expand their social justice work outside the classroom as activists, with students and on their own, to combat multiple forms of oppression.

While SJE is a distinct field, the term "social justice education" is often referred to as an "umbrella term" (Spalding, et al., 2010; Agarwal, et al., 2010; North, 2008) because there are many ways to center on issues of equity, access, power, and oppression. In fact, when scholars are invoking social justice education to redress these issues, they may just as often be adopting terminology, examples, or lessons from other fields such as critical pedagogy, culturally relevant, multicultural, anti-oppressive, anti-racist education as well as queer, woman, and disabilities studies, critical race theory, and critical pedagogy.

It is this inter-disciplinary nature of centering on issues of equity, access, power, and oppression that makes teaching itself, and teaching from a social justice perspective, a political act situated in cultural, racial, economic, political tensions (Freire, 1998; Montano, et al., 2002; McLaren, 2003; Cochran-Smith, et al., 2009; Schultz, 2008). As Cochran-Smith, et al. (2009) explain, "teaching for social justice [is] an activity with political dimensions in which all educators are responsible for challenging inequities in the social order and working with others to establish a more just society" (p. 352). In order to teach for social justice, educators must be able to recognize the highly political educational context that masquerades as neutral (Kumashiro, 2008; hooks, 1994; Zeichner, 1993), allowing reforms to act as gatekeepers for low-income students of Color in the name of meritocracy and common sense (Hursh, 2007; Kumashiro, 2008). In other words, educators themselves must have a political analysis of how inequality, oppression, and power operate as a starting place for social justice teaching.

The role of the teacher, therefore, is to contribute to the broader political project of identifying and eliminating oppression (Katsarou, et al., 2010) in order to work toward a more democratic society (Lipman, 2004; Freire, 1970; McDonald, 2007). Social justice educators are aware of social inequality and see themselves as responsible for playing a role in diminishing disparities within schools and the larger society (Cochran-Smith, et al., 2009; Giroux, 1988; Kincheloe, 2005; Schey & Uppstrom, 2009). Montano, et al. (2002) claim, "For critical educators, the concept of social justice is a foundation upon which to disrupt and change unjust, unequal, and undemocratic political institutions" (p. 266). They remind us that teachers must move beyond the surface interpretation of social justice in education as "community service days" or penny drives, and actively connect the concerns of students and their communities to the larger constructs of oppression in the form of racism, classism, gender subjugation, homophobia, ageism, and ableism (Katsarou, et al., 2010).

Struggling for Justice Both Inside and Outside of the Classroom (NYCoRE, 2003)

Because social justice educators are concerned with changing broader systems of oppression, they must be ready, willing, and able to work both inside and outside of their classrooms for social change. The work inside the classroom involves developing caring and respectful student relationships and culturally relevant curriculum and pedagogy that prepares students to create change. Outside of their classrooms, teachers must themselves take action to challenge oppressive systems that create educational and societal inequality (New York Collective of Radical Educators, 2003). Cochran-Smith, *et al.* (2009) provide a definition that addresses this dual nature of SJE: "Teaching for social justice is defined … by ensuring that all students have rich learning opportunities and challenging aspects of the system that reinforce inequities" (p. 374). To be fully realized social justice educators, teachers must be equally concerned with these dual goals if they hope to both educate their students and create actual change.

Inside the Classroom: Social Justice Pedagogy and Curriculum

Within the classroom domain, social justice educators challenge inequality through particular approaches that include 1) the relationships they develop with students, 2) the democratic classrooms they create, and 3) the specific ways in which they are then able to teach students to analyze and challenge oppression.

Social justice educators understand that developing caring relationships (Noddings, 1992; Valenzuela, 1999) with students based on a critical understanding of who students are and where they come from can lead to greater student academic success and leadership development (Cammarota & Romero, 2008). Therefore, social justice teachers take the time to get to know students' life circumstances (Tan, 2008) and the "broader social and economic forces that make learning difficult" (Cammarota & Romero, 2008, p. 467). This allows teachers to understand the challenges students face based on oppressive conditions these students may be experiencing, rather than rely on deficit notions of students' capacities. As North (2008) points out, social justice teachers "develop respect for individuals' differences and recognize how those differences might be informed by individuals' affiliations with particular social groups, such as those based on race, ethnicity, or class" (p. 422).

While these teachers understand the challenges students face in an unjust society, because they care about their students' success, they maintain high standards and don't allow these challenges to become excuses to teach less or to lower their expectations of students' capacities (Cochran-Smith, 2004; Ayers, 2008). Rather than see these issues as something beyond their control, social justice educators feel a responsibility to address these issues in solidarity with their students (Mikel & Hiserman, 2000) and use this knowledge as a basis for co-constructing curriculum and social action (Camangian, 2010; Duncan-Andrade & Morrell, 2008; Cochran-Smith,

2004). Social justice educators use students' home cultures to support academic success and to develop socio-cultural consciousness (Lipman, 2004; Schultz, 2008; Duncan-Andrade & Morrell, 2008; Camangian, 2010). Such teachers "draw on the talents and strengths that students bring to school (Nieto & Bode, 2008). This leads to greater trust, which ultimately allows for greater opportunities for students to take leadership for liberation (Cammarota & Romero, 2008).

Inside the classroom, these trusting relationships lay the foundation for democratic environments based on care, respect, and liberation that characterizes the classrooms of social justice educators. Such classrooms diminish traditional hierarchies between teacher and student, between those who have something to learn and those who have something to teach (Freire, 1970; Cammarota & Romero, 2008). Social justice educators reject the banking model of education, which posits students as empty vessels waiting to be filled (Freire, 1970). Instead, such educators cocreate transformative classroom communities where everyone feels the responsibility to contribute (hooks, 1994) and students take an active role in their own education (Hackman, 2005).

These democratic classrooms provide the setting in which educators engage students in developing analyses of oppression in a manner that is culturally relevant and action oriented. To do this successfully, first and foremost, social justice educators must have deep content knowledge and competence (Montano, et al., 2002) in order to help young people develop the academic literacy skills they need to navigate professional and civic life. Duncan-Andrade and Morrell (2008) explain:

> If these students are going to wear the mantle of the struggle for social and educational justice, if they are going to produce knowledge that forces us to look at our worlds differently, and if they are going to motivate people to act as collectives for social change, they will need to be able to read, write, and speak at high levels. (p. 129)

Duncan-Andrade and Morrell link academics to the struggle for justice and view academic skill development and content mastery as key components of social justice education and critical pedagogy. Hackman (2005) also describes three kinds of content mastery that social justice educators must possess: factual information, historical contextualization, and macro-to-micro content analysis. Without these areas of knowledge, Hackman (2005) suggests, educators will be unable to provide students with the necessary information and context to develop the skills described by Duncan-Andrade and Morrell (2008).

This content mastery across multiple disciplines is the foundation teachers use to teach the main theme of social justice education, which is to support students in developing political analyses of how oppression and inequality operate (Lipman, 2004). Moving away from a celebration of diversity and a focus on individuals, SJE concentrates on systems of oppression, power, and privilege, and the processes that perpetuate inequality (Hackman, 2005; Picower, 2011). SJE makes explicit parts of the curriculum that are often left hidden: "the inequities of society and institutional structures in which they are embedded" (Cochran-Smith, 2004, p. 78). By bringing to the surface the knowledge and history of people who have been marginalized and oppressed (McLaren, 2003; King, 2008), students are better able to understand how current conditions have been shaped by struggles for power. This provides them with a political analysis to better understand their own situations and how historical forces have shaped their lives. With these understandings, students are in a better position to act on injustice because they understand root causes of inequality and how they are perpetuated.

In addition to teaching the root causes of inequality and how they affect students' material conditions, SJE emphasizes teaching about social movements and the processes by which liberating change has happened (Hackman, 2005; Leistyna, 2008). This knowledge is shared so that, rather than feeling disempowered upon learning about systems of oppression (Hackman, 2005), students instead have the opportunity to understand that change is possible, and that ordinary people working in coalition have had powerful results. This lays the foundation for teachers and students to move outside the classroom to take action for social change themselves because they have role models of others who have done so (Cochran-Smith, 2004; Tan, 2008).

All of the work in the classroom, the relationships, democratic practices, and focus on redressing inequality, ultimately serves one purpose: providing students with the tools they need to take action for justice. As Westheimer and Suurtamm (2008) argue, the purpose of SJE is "to equip students with the knowledge, behavior, and skills needed to transform society into a place where social justice can exist" (p. 590). However, some of the literature that describes SJE stops short before explicating the role of actual action, promoting instead student skills and dispositions such as critical thinking, reflecting on their communities, developing agency, and the ability to act (Nieto & Bode, 2008). The development of these skills is critical, but to what end? The ultimate goal of SJE within the domain of the classroom is to allow students to apply their academic knowledge and skills to work toward changing social inequality and oppressive institutions (Westheimer & Kahne, 2007; Dixson & Smith, 2010), in order to "[transcend] and [transform] the struggles they experience in their everyday lives" (Camangian, 2008, p. 498). The goal is for students to move away from passivism and to become activists with the power to create change (Ayers, *et al.*, 2008; Christensen, 2009; Freire, 1970; Tan, 2008).

This inside the classroom section describes the work that social justice teachers do in terms of curriculum and instruction, and is often the first step on the road to becoming a fully realized social justice educator. Teacher education and professional development programs tend to provide some level of support for this inside the classroom work, focusing more on multicultural and culturally relevant curriculum development (Kailin, 2002; McDonald & Zeichner, 2008). However, SJE is incomplete without both teachers and students engaging in further action for change outside of the classroom because, as argued by the teacher activist group, NYCoRE (2001), "the struggle for justice does not end when the school bell rings."

Outside of the Classroom: Teacher Activism and Collective Organizing

All of the work that happens inside of the classroom is important and needs to take place in order to provide students with the knowledge and skills to create change. However, if SJE remains relegated to the classroom, there is little hope for a more just society to be realized. If educators continue to work as individuals within their classrooms, creating small democratic environments for a few students, they will never reach the ultimate goals of SJE because they will never impact the root causes of inequality.

Well-intentioned teachers who focus only on social justice curriculum and pedagogy are unable to reach larger goals of a more equitable society because they and their students will not actualize change. Racism, classism, patriarchy, and other forms of oppression may replicate themselves in the classroom but they did not start there. If no action is taken outside of the classroom, then the structures that perpetuate inequality are left untouched. Like a CD stuck on repeat, teachers who do not advocate for and engage in activism will have to reteach their lessons on inequality annually—however powerful and engaging—if they do not join any movements or contribute to actions that reshape the oppression they teach their students about.

Fully realized social justice educators have a responsibility to move beyond the inside the classroom role to engage in the second component of SJE, taking action to struggle for educational and broader justice (New York Collective of Radical Educators, 2003). This movement outside of the classroom expands the role from teacher to teacher activist. Recognizing that classrooms are reflections of broader societal injustice (Mikel & Hiserman, 2000), teacher activists step outside of the classroom to work for transformational change (Giroux, 1988; Kincheloe, 2005; McLaren, 2003). Such teachers not only teach about social issues and develop their students as activists, they also take on the role of activist directly. Montano, *et al.* (2002) rightly explain, "For these teachers, simply being a 'good' (that is, a social justice) teacher within the four walls of their own classrooms was not enough" (p. 272). Without enacting their own teacher activism, these teachers aren't creating social change. "A teacher activist criticizes those who are social justice teachers in thought only—who believe in the central tenets of critical pedagogy but who do not enact them in their own teaching and who are not active in social movements" (Montano, *et al.*, 2002, p. 266). Remaining within the safety or convenience of their classrooms, teachers leave SJE half done.

Teacher activists are of course interested in social justice pedagogy, but they are equally concerned with transforming both their schools and broader communities, and they engage in action in several ways: taking action alongside their students, challenging school and educational inequality, collaborating with parents and communities, and joining activist movements to take collective action. As Montano, *et al.* (2002) explain, a teacher activist, or organizer, is a fully realized social justice educator only when they begin walking the walk that they are promoting in their classroom:

"It is only through engagement in the practical and theoretical tasks of political activism that teacher activists begin to instantiate and make sense of their social justice philosophies and agendas" (p. 266). By expanding their actions beyond teaching about social issues to taking social action to transform injustice, social justice educators become teacher activists working to effect change rather than only teach about it.

The first dimension of teacher activism, working with students, has been touched upon in the discussion of what teachers can do within their classrooms. It is mentioned again here because this collaborative engagement blurs the line between what happens within and outside of classrooms. In this case, it refers to going beyond relying on students to take action by giving them social justice assignments such as writing letters or petitions. As a teacher activist, the role switch requires teachers to be "struggling alongside their students against oppressive conditions, both inside their classrooms and beyond the confines of the school in which they teach" (Montano, et al., 2002, p. 266). True social justice projects, as Cerecer, et al., (2010) remind us, cannot be single curricular activities, but rather "[need] to include students and adults, as well as the school-wide and local community" (p. 157). Rather than seeing their role as teachers who are supporting students to do social justice work, teacher activists roll up their sleeves and get to work alongside students, because they see themselves as equal partners struggling together toward the same outcome.

Working explicitly on issues of educational justice is another way in which teachers move beyond their classroom door to increase educational opportunities for their students (Kapustka, et al., 2009; Cochran-Smith, et al., 2009; Chubbuck, 2010; Westheimer & Kahne, 2007). From fighting oppressive policies such as high-stakes testing, school funding, and undemocratic educational structures, social justice teachers concern themselves with both school site issues and broader local and national educational issues that impact academic opportunity and equity. Often starting with school-based committee involvement, teacher activists routinely expand this dimension of outside of the classroom justice work to broader educational organizing.

Whether working on issues of educational equity or broader social justice issues, such as political economic conditions that maintain inequality like housing costs, gentrification, and minimum-wage policies (Anyon, 2005), such teachers work in collaboration with other educators, students, their families, and communities (Cochran-Smith, 2004; Bigelow, et al., 1994). Teacher activists have two important understandings about change: 1) isolated teachers acting alone cannot put sufficient pressure on systems to create change and 2) the process of how change is brought about is equally important to the product, therefore change best happens in a democratic way, in which all stakeholders—including parents, students, and community members—have a voice in the outcome. This understanding of shared democratic change motivates teacher activists to engage in the often difficult and politically nuanced work of building coalitions with parent, youth, community, and union groups working toward similar goals.

Since isolated teachers acting alone cannot have enough impact, another distinction of fully developed teacher activism is that action is taken collectively rather than individually. In contrast, often when teachers attempt to engage in social change, they typically do so as individual teachers. Marshall and Anderson (2009) interviewed 52 activist educators to learn about their work and found that the teachers in their study often acted behind the scenes as individuals. These activist educators were not part of larger networks or movements with other like-minded educators and Marshall and Anderson (2009) suggested that they might benefit from such a community. Carlson (1987) critiqued the "individual" nature of teachers who do become political actors, and quotes Jean Anyon to point out that, "[w]hile accommodation and resistance as modes of daily activity provide ... ways of negotiating individually felt social conflict or oppression, this individual activity of everyday life remains just that: individual, fragmented, and isolated from group effort. It is thus politically weakened" (as cited in Carlson, 1987, p. 295).

To strengthen the impact of teacher activism, social justice educators need to be politically engaged in sustained and collective ways. As Montano, *et al.* (2002) argue, "many social justice educators are, in fact, teacher activists in political and social movements working to bring about changes in educational policies that they perceive to be unjust" (p. 265). Many such teachers have been creating and finding homes in grassroots teacher activist groups that have been organizing themselves in cities across the United States (Network of Teacher Activist Groups, n.d.). These groups of teachers situate their work in relation to broader social justice movements and unabashedly embrace the political nature of teaching and education, working collectively to promote the broader involvement of teachers in urban public school systems by engaging in activities ranging from anti-war activism to social justice curriculum writing. These teachers have embraced both tenets of social justice education by working both inside and outside of their classrooms. They help students develop political analyses and activist opportunities while also working outside of the classroom to create impactful change on oppressive institutions.

Sequence of the Book

As laid out in the definition of SJE and teacher activism, I argue that to actualize liberatory change, social justice educators must work both inside and outside of the classroom. Most teachers, however, do not enter the field with this vision of their role. As most teacher educators with a social justice lens can attest to, many teachers enter the field with little to no recognition that social inequality exists, and therefore they are not motivated to work to change a system that they see as functioning equitably. This book addresses barriers to the development of teacher activism by identifying ideologies such as this that many teachers hold about both injustice and activism, and the tools they use to subvert, discredit, and avoid challenges to their understandings about oppression and social change. Based on original research on three different groups of teachers—1) pre-service teachers actively opposed to social justice, 2) emerging social justice educators, and 3) experienced teacher activists—this book traces a continuum of development toward activism as teachers overcome the barriers and roadblocks along the way. By understanding these barriers, pre-service and in-service teachers along with teacher educators will be in a better position to develop the kind of political analysis that lays the foundation for teacher activism.

This first chapter set up the definition of what social justice education is. Because the term has been used many different ways and risks co-optation, it is important that I clarify the way it is referred to in this book. The remainder of the book looks in detail at the challenges of moving teachers at various stages of political consciousness to enact the vision of teaching laid out in this chapter that includes working both inside and outside of the classroom.

One of the first barriers to SJE is the disconnect between the life experiences of the teaching force, primarily White, middle-class women, and the students whom they teach. Chapter 2, "'Why Do We Have to Talk about Race Again?': Oppositional Stances and Tools of Whiteness," focuses on original research with White pre-service teachers. It demonstrates how their life experiences influence them to have problematic assumptions about students of Color, urban schools, and communities. Because these teachers believe the United States is already relatively equitable and that Whites are the real victims of racism, they see no need to become educators who would change the conditions that are already working for them. This way of seeing the world limits their ability to become social justice educators because they do not have the foundation needed: the political analysis to recognize inequality and the desire to act upon it. This chapter examines such oppositional pre-service teachers' responses to challenges to their problematic assumptions and discusses how these responses are much more threatening than simple resistance or isolated comments. The chapter also provides some strategies for teacher educators and professional developers to consider using to interrupt these assumptions.

Fortunately, not all teachers come to the profession with this level of resistance to developing a framework of justice. Chapter 3, "Teaching for Justice: Developing Strategies for Integrating SJE in the Classroom," examines original research with a second set of teachers: emerging educators who volunteered to participate in a social justice critical inquiry project (CIP). Unlike the teachers in Chapter 2, these teachers began to recognize inequality and sought avenues to teach about it. They developed strategies to integrate their developing political analysis into their classroom teaching. By using these strategies, the teachers were successful in creating classrooms where students learned about social issues, even in settings that were not supportive of this stance. However, the teachers struggled to take the next step of moving outside of their classroom as teacher activists because their strategies were limited to their classrooms, leaving larger issues of social injustice untouched.

Chapter 4, "Stuck at the Classroom Door: Falling Back on Tools of Inaction," continues the journey with the CIP teachers as they gained a few more years of experience. The next logical step in the CIP members' development as social justice educators would have been to start to directly address issues of inequality by moving outside of the classroom door to engage their students in social action and to develop as activists themselves. However, this proved difficult. This chapter, based on data from the third year of CIP, examined what happened as these teachers began to realize the enormity of the challenge of moving outside of their classroom to create social change. These teachers had two choices: 1) to embrace the difficulty of the challenge and dedicate themselves to growing both as teachers and activists, or 2) to retreat back to the comfort of the classroom. In an attempt to not feel like failures in their journey, the teachers instead used what I call "Tools of Inaction" to try to relieve the tension they felt by not taking their next steps. Explored in detail, these tools served to postpone, justify, or redirect the responsibility of becoming active in struggling for sustainable social change as teacher activists.

In contrast to the CIP teachers who used the Tools of Inaction to diminish the discomfort of complacency, Chapter 5, "Reconciling the Vision: Taking Action for Educational Justice," looks at teachers who work to reconcile their vision of social justice and the reality of public schooling in the United States. The findings in this chapter are based on a national study of teacher activists who actively work in collective social justice teacher groups. These teachers understand that education functions in two ways, as both a space for potential liberation and as force of injustice that reproduces and reinforces existing social inequality. These teachers worked to address both of these functions. To create liberating spaces, they taught students to develop a critical analysis of their world and provided them with opportunities to take action. To battle against oppression, the teacher activists organized collectively to stand up to injustice and to get teachers' voices into policy arenas. This chapter highlights two concrete examples of teachers enacting this vision in Tucson, Arizona, in the battle for ethnic studies and in Milwaukee, Wisconsin, where teachers struggled for workers' rights.

The final chapter, Chapter 6: "'Making a Difference': Teaching in the Classroom and Organizing in the Streets," argues that for teachers to realize their expressed desire to "make a difference" in their students' lives, they must take action both inside and outside of the classroom. The journey toward teacher activism may not be linear, but it does require being able to understand inequality, social change, and social justice in particular ways. This chapter further explores these steps toward activism and why teacher organizing is critically important in our current historical context.

My Path

In many ways, my own journey as a social justice educator and teacher activist mirrors the flow of this book. The book looks at a continuum of social justice development moving from teachers who hold mainstream ideologies about race to teachers who are motivated to teach about social justice and then on to activist teachers who actively seek opportunities to create change. Unwittingly, this is very much the progression I went through myself as I developed as a social justice educator.

Like the teachers in Chapter 2, growing up as a White girl in more privileged settings, I certainly was not immune from being socialized to have particular understandings of race and difference. However, I feel that a variety of life experiences, or "critical race moments," mitigated the impact of this socialization, which in turn motivated me to seek out different opportunities that put me on a path toward social justice activism. I share some of these below, not to paint a portrait of myself as a "White exception," but to show that particular experiences have the potential to interrupt the internalization of hegemonic understandings. Attempting to recognize and replicate similar mitigating factors has shaped the way I prepare teachers, and has led me to provide my students with opportunities to wrestle with similar experiences.

One prerequisite to teaching for social justice is recognizing that racism exists and that it benefits White people. As shown in Chapter 2, many White teachers do not recognize this to be the case. What, unfortunately, helped me to see that racism exists was the differential treatment between myself and my childhood best friend, Jasmine, a Puerto Rican student who was one of the few students of Color at our predominately White private school. Jasmine, a math wiz, basically carried me through elementary school mathematics. When we entered middle school and our school started ability tracking, I was placed in Math B, and Jasmine, surprisingly, was placed in Math C. Her parents fought the school administration, who told them it was for her own good. Because of her parents' continued resistance, though, the school eventually placed Jasmine in Math B, where they kept her for another year until she was rightfully promoted to Math A. Jasmine's math misplacement is but one example of the school and teachers treating Jasmine in ways that I wasn't treated. Because Jasmine was my "bff," I naturally had empathy for her and anger about the situation that changed the way I saw seemingly "neutral" educational decisions.

Another key factor in being an ally in the struggle for justice is recognizing that, as a White person, you don't have all the answers and that it is necessary to listen to communities of Color about what is needed. This was a more difficult understanding for me to gain because of the way my school and surroundings structured experiences that placed me in the "savior" role. Because of the situations with Jasmine, I recognized inequality and was motivated to do something about it. I was active in the school's social service program and participated in many activities such as tutoring in homeless shelters in East Harlem and the Lower East Side, neighborhoods the school considered "dangerous." The programs I volunteered in were run by White adults who insisted on calling cabs for me when I would leave in the evening. This didn't make me feel safe; rather, it made me feel extremely embarrassed, and I knew there was something wrong with the fact that I was being shuttled out of a place where the 8-year-olds I was tutoring had to stay.

At the time, I didn't have the words or theoretical understanding of why I felt this way or why this was problematic: I simply felt uncomfortable. These experiences were meant to reinforce the problematic assumptions that people of Color are in need of help and that "nice, White girls" like myself were considered to be in the position to "help," even though I wasn't really bringing any special training to the table. Even though I was positioned in this way, unlike the women profiled in Chapter 2, I was able to resist this role to a degree because of this unnamable discomfort that led me to make different choices in the future.

At the same time, motivated by romantic notions of the "sixties," I started to dip my toes in some of the activism happening in New York City in the late 1980s. Somehow I ended up at a local socialist organization meeting (don't ask me how, I have no idea), and started going to protests in front of Shell, Mobil, and Exxon to get them to divest from South Africa. I marched with César Chávez to get "poison grapes" out of local grocery stores—although I had no idea who he was at the time other than a "nice man who came all the way from California to march with us!" At the time, I saw myself as a social justice activist—I was showing up and yelling and marching. In retrospect, however, I really didn't know what I was doing because I didn't have a fully formed political analysis of how inequality operated.

It wasn't until I took classes as an undergraduate that gave me a framework to understand oppression that I would really be able to move out of this period of an outward "performance" of social justice activism that will be further discussed in Chapter 4. While my activism at this stage was incomplete, these early experiences did instill in me the understanding that if you don't like something that is happening in the world, you can do something about it. This is an important motivator for taking action toward social justice.

After high school, I was an undergraduate in the early 1990s in Ann Arbor, Michigan, during a time when the United States was going through a series of racially charged events. I wanted to continue to work with children, but, motivated by my discomfort with the settings I worked at in high school, I sought a program that had leadership of Color rather than "well-intentioned" White adults. I ended up at the Peace Neighborhood Center, a community center that served the residents of the city's low-income housing communities, and this served as probably the most significant period of development of my racial consciousness. These housing communities were literally hidden from most of Ann Arbor, built around the outskirts of the city and off of all the main roads—most people on campus had no idea they existed. I was one of the only people who wasn't either African American or raised in the community that worked there. My co-workers and I weren't colorblind to the differences; we recognized and joked around about them, making it a setting in which I felt at ease and welcomed. Fortunately, this experience extinguished any remnant of the "savior" role I carried because it was clear that the leadership had more of the "answers" than I ever could have brought, and they were generous in training me to be successful in working with the young people at the center.

Being at the Peace Neighborhood Center during this time period allowed me to reshape my racial lens because I was exposed to the unfiltered views of my co-workers on racially charged topics. For instance, before the students came for the afterschool program that I co-directed, the staff and adults whose needs were being met by the center would hang around in the main room and watch TV. Because this was the early 1990s, day in and day out we were glued to the TV news, first watching the Rodney King incident, and subsequent LA uprising, then tuning in to and analyzing the Clarence Thomas–Anita Hill hearings. Finally, we watched the speeding white Bronco and the daily developments of the O.J. trial. Being a part of the discussions and listening to the uncensored reactions of the Black people around me was just part of my daily life, and their reactions became part of my own perspective. Having opportunities to develop meaningful relationships with people of Color, hearing and learning from their perspectives on issues of race, feeling comfortable participating in racially charged discussions, and working in an environment that was run by members of the community being served all played a significant role in shaping my political analysis. As will be seen in Chapter 2, many White people either do not have, or actively avoid, settings in which they will be the minority, and therefore do not have the experiences in which they can build similar understandings.

After a move to California and several other working experiences that explicitly focused on race, equality, and education, I decided to become a classroom teacher. As luck would have it, the Oakland Unified School District placed me at Prescott Elementary, the school that had gained national attention by being the "Ebonics school." Race was always on the table, and much of the professional development provided focused on learning more about African American culture and making connections to the classroom. Because of my prior experiences, I was used to being around Black people talking about racism, and, unlike some of the other White teachers at the school, I embraced the culturally focused professional development opportunities. The veteran Black teachers led by Carrie Secret trained me how to integrate both issues of culture and the social issues that I was already passionate about into the classroom curriculum. At this point in my life, my teaching was similar to the teachers in Chapter 3 as I was learning the concrete skills of being a social justice educator inside of the classroom. While I was still somewhat active in broader issues of equity and educational policy, it took a back seat while I learned how to create culturally relevant and social justice curriculum.

When I moved back to New York and was working on my dissertation, I was introduced to NYCoRE, and it was by joining this group that I was able to pull together my inside and outside of the classroom work. Granted, by this time, my "classroom" was at the university level, preparing people to be elementary school teachers. Like the teacher activists in Chapter 5, becoming active in a group setting provided me with a place to integrate my desire to prepare people to create liberatory classroom environments while also taking action to change conditions and policies that were increasing inequality. Having a supportive space of like-minded, committed educators who shared my passion for educational justice has both strengthened and pushed my work and my sense of efficacy. This journey of development and constant learning continues to unfold for myself and the teachers profiled in this book.

While there isn't a one-to-one correspondence between my experiences and other people's journeys toward social justice activism, it is clear that there are stages that people go through where they gain the mindsets and skillsets that are needed for fully realized teacher activism: awareness, empathy, analysis, and action. The heart of this book is to help teachers recognize where they are in this continuum and to provide them with some insights into how to continue to move forward. For me, being a teacher activist shapes the way I see and interact with the world in a way that makes me feel hopeful instead of hopeless. As activist and poet Staceyann Chin says, "Every day I get better at knowing that it is not a choice to be an activist; rather, it is the only way to hold on to the better parts of my human self. It is the only way I can live and laugh without guilt" (Goodreads, n.d.). My hope with this book is that it can support educators toward teacher activism so that they can teach "without guilt," knowing that they are doing their part to ameliorate the injustices that unequal education reproduces.

2

"WHY DO WE HAVE TO TALK ABOUT RACE AGAIN?"

Oppositional Stances and Tools of Whiteness

Teacher activism necessitates the ability for educators to engage on three levels that they may not be predisposed to think about. The first is having a recognition and political analysis of injustice and how it operates to create and maintain oppression on multiple levels. The second is the willingness and ability to integrate this analysis into academic teaching in the classrooms. The third is to have the mindset and skillset to expand their social justice work outside the classroom, with students and on their own, to stand up to oppression. This chapter explores the implications of the "unexamined Whiteness of teaching" (Picower, 2007) and its impact on teachers' ability and willingness to engage on these three levels. Tracing teachers' identities and life experiences, and the impact they have on their understanding of people different than themselves, this chapter demonstrates how the socialization of some White teachers blocks their ability to recognize inequality, let alone teach or take action to combat it—which is the foundation of social justice education (SJE). By using "Tools of Whiteness" designed to protect their previously socialized understandings, the teachers in this chapter maintain their racist ideology, ensuring their inability to move toward teacher activism.

This chapter examines research done with a group of pre-service female teachers in their twenties who were graduate students of mine in a course on multicultural education for elementary classrooms. The course, collaboratively designed with a colleague, was intended to help teachers begin exploring their own racial identity and class privilege, their assumptions about students of Color and the communities that they come from, and their developing understandings of the role of the teacher in urban schools. Students went through a process of reflecting on their life experiences and the ways in which those experiences influenced their role as future teachers.

Due to a variety of unusual scheduling dilemmas, this particular semester, I only had ten students enrolled in the course, and all of them were White. This presented a unique opportunity to look specifically at the role that Whiteness played in their conceptions of students of Color and teaching in urban communities. Through course sessions, individual interviews, and course work, I collected data that uncovered how these women's racial identity influenced their conceptions of themselves, their students, and teaching, as well as how they responded to concepts that challenged their preconceived notions about people of Color and urban communities.

The course included a variety of readings,[1] exercises, videos, and assignments designed to help students develop knowledge and understanding of the dimensions of identity, including race, ethnicity, religion, gender, sexual orientation, socio-economic class, and their impact on school achievement and experiences. Students examined the roles of identity, power, and privilege in their respective educational experiences in order to better understand their relationship to their future students. In keeping with the traditions of critical multiculturalism, the course "examine[d] Whiteness, its privilege, normativity (its ability to designate itself as the standard) and erasure. It induce[d] White people to rethink their understanding of their own ethnicity and the construction of their consciousness" (Kincheloe & Steinberg, 1997, p. 30). One of the main goals of the course was for students to engage in ongoing reflection about their personal philosophy and their commitment to SJE.

The life experiences of these teachers influenced them to have problematic assumptions about urban students, schools, and communities. Through under-standings passed on and reinforced by their families, friends, and schooling, the participants believed many negative stereotypes about people of Color—stereotypes often characterized by fear and a sense of deficiency. As part of an ongoing cycle of racism, participants carried these misconceptions from their childhood into their preparation for the classroom. These assumptions provided the basis for hegemonic understandings about the students and families the participants worked with in their student teaching placements; these are explored in more detail in the next section.

Hegemonic Understandings

Two main hegemonic stories emerged that were used to maintain my students' initial beliefs about people of Color. The term "hegemonic understandings" refers to the students' internalized ways of making meaning about how society is organized. Their two main hegemonic understandings, 1) fear and 2) victimization, emerged out of their life experiences and their perceptions about their interactions with individuals of other races. Their hegemonic understandings of fear constructed people of Color, particularly African Americans, as "scary" and violent. Their vic-timization stories positioned Whites as the new recipients of racism who were unfairly losing rights and resources that were being given to people of Color. Their views of people of Color as both dangerous and simultaneously taking what was rightfully theirs were used to justify their willful lack of understanding about how racial inequality operated.

Hegemonic Understanding #1: Fear

Fear was by far the most prevalent hegemonic story shared. These pre-service teachers expressed a sense of anxiety in situations with people of Color, largely based on stereotypes from early influences from their family and the media. This anxiety was escalated to a sense of terror in the few situations in which they found themselves to be the only White people. With only a few exceptions, all of their stories involved African Americans as dangerous criminals who violated the pre-service teachers' sense of safety. Diane's response echoed others when she described the high school in the town next to her predominately White community:

> We always knew that was the high school that was always in trouble. That was the high school that had really big Black football players. ... I mean my friends in general didn't want to go to their school for sports events because it was a little scary. Scary like their attitude and stuff was different—seemed to be different than ours—and their behaviors and stuff seemed to be different than ours, so we avoided it. ... I think that you are always going to have those feelings.

In this example, Diane relied on a number of common generalizations about Black teens based on her sense of how they were different from her friends and therefore dangerous. She continued:

> If I'm walking home and there is a big group of Black guys walking towards me—I'm probably going to cross the street. I don't know if it's the same if it was a group of White guys. Like it would depend on their attitudes and things like that and how they are dressed. ... I mean I guess we assume that if a guy is dressed in a suit or whatever that they must be perfectly fine whereas if they are wearing big jeans then they are not fine. You know? It's more professional I guess. Because you always hear about baggy jeans and hoodlums and then you think, "well—he must be!"

Here, Diane's childhood conceptualization of African American teenagers has carried into her adult understandings of Black men. Her fear remained based in her construction of "different" as "dangerous" as these are the markers she used to make her stereotypical judgments. Of particular interest was her use of pronouns to create a sense of collusion with her ideas. For example, she said, "I think *you* are always going to have those feelings" and "I mean *we* assume that if a guy is dressed ... " These pronouns allowed her to avoid taking ownership over these stereotypes and to position herself within a broader White collective that presumably shared her stance.

As future teachers, these constructions of people of Color impact their understandings of their students. In describing her concerns about teaching in her classroom placement at an urban elementary school with predominately students of Color, Diane shared:

> That some of them [the students] are a lot bigger than me. Like some of the toughness of some of the boys I guess. Some of the boys are like tough! And that's scary for me. [I'm scared that] a fight would break out in class I guess … like either they would come at me, or that I couldn't stop it. I mean I'm a small person and like I'm in a third-grade classroom and some of the boys are the same height as me. It's intimidating.

Diane, who stated that she would cross the street when a group of African American men shared the sidewalk with her, made clear that this fear did not leave her at the classroom door. Her hegemonic understandings of Black men as violent and criminal shaped her understandings and fears of 8-year-old children from whom she may not be able to defend herself against in an anticipated attack. These understandings of Blackness as dangerous tainted her ability to develop empathy for her students of Color and their families, which blocked her willingness to recognize larger systems of racial inequality. In her view, Diane is the victim of oppression, as she is the one who has to teach these rough and intimidating children. This ideology is explored further in the next section.

Diane, who adhered to a personal definition of racism, believed it results not in negative outcomes for people of Color, but rather in low self-esteem and the tendency to stereotype among people of Color:

> They [African Americans] won't have very good feelings about themselves if they're always told, you know, like "they're bad" or whatever so they don't try to—or maybe they try even harder to prove everybody wrong … I mean, I talked about the idea of a group of like Black—I mean African American kids—walking down the street, like if I were to cross the street would they think that it's because like, I was just crossing the street, or you know to purposely walk away from them? So would they assume the worst about me even if maybe that wasn't my first thought?

Diane's response is intriguing on a number of levels. She locates the suffering of racism within the psyche of people of Color, negating the existence of structural or material oppression. She attributes African Americans' work ethic to their low self-esteem, blaming people of Color for their resulting positions by ignoring structural barriers they may face. Diane had previously admitted that she crosses the street because she is scared of sharing the sidewalk with African American men. Now she claimed that perhaps she is innocently "just crossing the street," but, because of their tendency to make assumptions, African Americans might think she is a racist as a result. This way of seeing the world maintained her problematic assumptions because Diane, the White woman, becomes the victim of her own racism. This hegemonic understanding blocks the development of a deeper political analysis that recognizes racism operating on multiple levels. Without this understanding of how oppression functions, these teachers have no reason to act against something they won't admit exists.

Hegemonic Understanding #2: Whites as Victims

The teachers in this study often used their White ethnic backgrounds to create a hegemonic story about how people of Color should be able to pick themselves up by their bootstraps. Dawn called upon her Italian family's immigration experience to justify her resentment towards people of Color:

> Like when my dad came here to America, he had a lot of struggle. He started working when he was 10 years old, and he didn't know a word of English. He pulled himself up and he worked hard. He doesn't now go back to the people who wouldn't give him a job—and those were the non-White people! He had to go through his family—and his family lived in a very small apartment in Brooklyn, couldn't afford a thing and, you know, he got over it. And he is over it now.

Dawn described her father's experience of the American dream: he came here with nothing, worked hard, and made it. Here the implication is clear—if he could make it, anyone can. She used her family's Italian immigration story as the normative experience upon which all people should model success. Such a view upholds the dominant ideology of people of Color as lazy and victims of their circumstances, and helps teachers such as Dawn to perpetuate the myth of American meritocracy. With no recognition of institutional racism, her assumption is that all people operate on a level playing field with equal opportunity for success. She continued to connect the dots between her family's experiences and how that affected her thinking about people of Color:

> This is where I am feeling a little bit nervous. Like maybe I'm almost being a little bit racist because you just want to say sometimes [shouting] "Get over it! Like get over it! It's 2000 [something], get over it! You know, move on!" So what you're Black, so what I'm White—if I get better grades in school—maybe I worked harder. You know, if I get a job, maybe I deserved it! Why does it always have to be like, [whiny voice] "Well, they're the minority, let's give it to them." I'm done with that, it's time to start a new life.

While she did wonder if she was being "a little bit racist," she believed that the American meritocracy was working fine—she deserved what she has because she worked harder—until affirmative action came along and society started distributing resources to minorities, presumably resources that should belong to her.

Dawn used her family history to attempt to show the ways in which they themselves, rather than people of Color, were the real victims of racism. When asked for examples of racism that they had seen or heard, the participants in this study typically shared stories in which White people had been verbally or physically attacked by people of Color. One such story stemmed from the sense that Whites are being taken advantage of as a result of affirmative action. Dawn, for example, had an intense and angry response to the concept of White privilege:

> Every time [author Gary Howard] said the word *privilege*; that just drove me crazy. Like today—I'm White, so that means I have to pay full tuition. I don't get it. I mean when we go to college we have to check off what race you are and I hate to say it but if you are African American or Hispanic—you get looked at first. I mean this really pisses me off. We don't have privilege anymore—they do. And they keep going back to saying, [whining] "Well—we had a bad life in the past." You weren't around then—ya know!

Dawn drew on the dominant narrative of reverse racism to explain why she was victimized by affirmative action, claiming that people of Color are actually more privileged than White people. She did not veil the anger she felt about this loss of privilege and made clear she felt that any past injustice others might have faced has no impact on present circumstances.

Influenced by their life experiences, participants either created or bought into mainstream hegemonic stories that constructed White people as the true victims of racism. Because these stories were so tightly interwoven into who they were, the teachers were highly committed to maintaining these understandings. These stories blocked pre-service teachers' abilities to even acknowledge that racism existed. Because they would not recognize racism, or saw themselves as the victims of it, they lacked the motivation or the analytical foundation to work toward a more equitable society. Without these prerequisites, these future educators were light years from having the ability to teach for social justice. Take Dawn's sense of victimization for example. Her understanding of people of Color as coming up ahead in what she saw as the zero-sum game of racism (Norton & Sommers, 2011) blocked her ability to understand that, in fact, people of Color suffer from institutional racism in the field of education. Without this understanding, she had no ability to teach her students about issues of race, let alone any desire to attempt to improve educational opportunities for the very people she saw as victimizing herself and her family.

Since these stories impede pre-service teachers' ability to teach and work toward activism, as a professor committed to preparing social justice educators, I found it necessary to try to disrupt these understandings. In the next section, I examine what happened when class activities were offered to help disrupt these hegemonic stories. The students used a number of oppositional stances and Tools of Whiteness as defensive mechanisms to preserve their incoming stories. The use of these hegemonic understandings prevented these pre-service teachers from beginning the journey toward

SJE because they continued to deny either the existence of or their connection to racial inequality, which in turn made the idea of SJE out of the question.

Oppositional Stances and Tools of Whiteness

With hegemonic understandings of fear and White victimhood as starting points, the participants in this study enrolled in a course on multicultural education that I taught, designed to interrogate their understandings about race and equity. The course provided an introduction to the foundations of multicultural, culturally relevant education focused on the concepts of oppression and privilege. As the pre-service negotiated the challenges presented by reflecting upon their prior knowledge about race and difference, they enacted a range of oppositional stances and called upon a variety of Tools of Whiteness used to maintain their prior hegemonic understandings.

These oppositional stances are representative of a range of responses that many pre-service teachers have when they realize they are expected to teach from a multicultural or social justice perspective. These stances include denying the existence of racism, refuting their own connection to it, blaming others, refusing to take responsibility, and adopting a missionary stance. Students' negative reactions to multicultural education are typically referred to as *resistance* in the literature on White teachers and multicultural education. I contend, however, that these stances are not simply a passive resistance but much more of an active protection of their hegemonic stories and White supremacy.

Each oppositional stance, and associated Tool of Whiteness, serves to block particular understandings of race that are needed to move toward SJE. Only by removing those blocks can teachers develop the analysis needed to move along their journey. In my experience as a teacher educator, I have found that many students like the ones highlighted in this study are lacking two prerequisites for beginning the journey toward SJE: 1) empathy with people suffering under oppressive circumstances and 2) historical and current knowledge about how inequality operates.

For those concerned with preparing or supporting social justice educators, understanding these oppositional stances can help us to be more strategic in how we attempt to loosen some teachers' hegemonic understandings about race. While many of the participants in this study adopted several of these stances at once or moved between them fluidly, each stance represents a particular (mis)understanding about race. By pinpointing these (mis)understandings and how teachers actively attempt to maintain them, we are more capable of choosing activities, readings, films, or strategies designed to hone in on that specific issue.

As seen in Table 2.1, pre-service teachers often rely on five oppositional stances that are backed by particular Tools of Whiteness:

"It ain't broke, so there's nothing to fix" is adopted when pre-service teachers
    attempt to deny the very existence of racism. This stance is supported by Tools of
    Whiteness that perpetuate their understanding that people of Color are
    complaining about something that no longer exists.
"Hey—don't look at me!" is a stance used to refute teachers' connection to, or their
    role in, the cycle of racism and is buttressed by tools that help them to feel that racism is
    either a problem of the past or that it has nothing to do with them personally.
The "I play by the rules" stance maintains their innocence by allowing the user to
    explain all the ways they are a "good person." This allows them to point their
    fingers at the "real" perpetuators of racism, people who are overtly racist.
"What do you expect me to do about it?" is adopted when the user begins to
    recognize that racism exists but they want to deflect any responsibility for having
    to do anything about it. It is backed by tools that justify their sense of being too
    overwhelmed or unequipped to deal with it.
"Here I come to save the day!" is adopted when teachers recognize racism but
    develop inappropriate, missionary ideals to try to "save" people of Color from
    themselves. Based in deficit notions of people of Color, this stance and
    supporting tools ignore institutional racism and position the user as a hero who
    can magically uplift people from their circumstances.

Each oppositional stance represents a particular way of thinking about race.
Denying the existence of racism, refuting their personal connection, pointing the
finger, deflecting responsibility, and becoming missionaries are the basic five oppositional stances that occurred. Each one of those stances was manifested with particular discursive scripts that repeated themselves and were echoed by multiple
participants. These reoccurring stances maintained their hegemonic understandings.

TABLE 2.1 Oppositional Stances

1) It ain't broke, so there's nothing to fix
    - Denies the very existence of racism
    - People of Color are complaining about something that no longer exists
2) Hey—don't look at me!
    - Refutes teachers' connection to their own role in the cycle of racism
    - Racism has nothing to do with them personally
3) I play by the rules
    - Positions the user as a "good person"
    - Points the finger at others, who are the "real" perpetrators of racism
4) What do you expect me to do about it?
    - Recognizes that racism exists, but deflects any personal responsibility to do anything
      about it
5) Here I come to save the day!
    - Recognizes that racism exists, but uses inappropriate, missionary ideals to try to "save"
      people of Color

TABLE 2.2 Oppositional Stances and Tools of Whiteness

Oppositional stances	It ain't broke, so there's nothing to fix	Hey—don't look at me!	I play by the rules	What do you expect me to do about it?	Here I come to save the day!
Tools of Whiteness	Now that things are equal	I never owned a slave	I don't make racist comments	Out of my control	I just want to help them
	Don't bring up the past	Stop making me feel guilty	I don't talk about race	I can't relate	
	Protect the innocent	It's not like I live in a mansion	I don't even see color		
		Everyone's oppressed somehow	I'm nice to everyone		
			I would kiss a Black guy		

In the construction of these stances, the participants repeated almost scripted responses to maintain their incoming understandings. As seen in Table 2.2, I've called these repeated scripts "Tools of Whiteness" because they function to preserve hierarchies of power with Whites at the top. Tools allow a job to be done more effectively or efficiently; Tools of Whiteness facilitate in the job of maintaining and supporting hegemonic stories and oppositional stances, which, in turn, uphold structures of White supremacy. In an attempt to preserve their hegemonic understandings, participants used these tools to deny, evade, subvert, or avoid the issues raised. Taken together, these stances and tools block teachers' ability or willingness to teach from a social justice perspective as teacher activists.

Oppositional Stance #1: It Ain't Broke, So There's Nothing to Fix

The "It ain't broke, so there's nothing to fix" stance is adopted to insist that racism is a thing of the past that has been solved. The stance posits that inequality in general doesn't target any particular group, and, if it did, it is really White people that are mainly the victims. It is supported through the use of three particular Tools of Whiteness: "Now that things are equal," "Don't bring up the past," and "Protect the innocent." Since, in this stance, everyone is equal and people deserve their station in life, why in the world would there be a need to change the world?

"Now That Things Are Equal"

By claiming that the United States made progress on race relations, the teachers used the "Now that things are equal" tool to dismiss the importance or negate the existence of racism. This tool functions to maintain problematic assumptions by implying that people of Color are "playing the race card" when they complain about something that does not exist, particularly in light of the common notion that Whites are the real victims of racism. As Dawn stated in a conversation in which someone brought up the concept of reparations:

> Like there were laws made and Ruby Bridges came along and she changed everything and you know there was that teacher that said "let's make a change." … And now we are all going into the classroom we are going to make things a little more better because we are becoming educated in what to do in the classroom, so I don't really think we have to say the words "I'm sorry."

The implication of Dawn's statement is that now that things are "more better," the need for continued anti-racist work is unnecessary as people of Color have more power in society and are subsequently victimizing Whites. The tool of "Now that things are equal" protected her hegemonic story of White innocence in racism and her understanding that people of Color are undeservingly taking what rightfully belongs to Whites through affirmative action. Since Whites are perceived to be the real victims, it's inconceivable and even offensive to teachers with this oppositional stance to be expected to teach about racism. Norton and Sommers (2011) demonstrate that Whites believe that racism is a zero-sum game and that the progress made on racism against Blacks has come at the expense of Whites—so why should teachers like Dawn address a problem that no longer exists, and worse that targets her?! Because SJE is predicated on making special efforts to overcome historic inequalities, the use of this tool ensures that teachers will not recognize racism or teach from such a perspective.

"Don't Bring up the Past"

White teachers such as Dawn become angry when people of Color (and anti-racist Whites) bring up issues of racism. Like "Now that things are equal," this tool upholds the oppositional stance "It ain't broke, so there's nothing to fix" because racism is over, so just stop talking about it already! "Don't bring up the past" served as role reversal consistent with Dawn's problematic assumptions that blamed people of Color for their marginalization and positioned Whites as victims of racism. Dawn reflected:

> I just get along with people, like if they're nice or whatever, I'll be like friends with them. But once they start bringing up the past! And I love listening about culture and I love teaching my students about culture, but once they start blaming me and making me feel guilty, that's what makes me angry!

Dawn's use of the tool "Don't bring up the past" served to negate the idea that historic racism affects the current context. She revealed her rules about the role of culture and people of Color—just be nice, don't discuss racism, focus on "culture." This tool deflects the possibility of exploring the role that historical racism may play in today's society, allowing teachers to believe there is nothing broken with current racial hierarchies.

The most prevalent form of "Don't bring up the past" deals with the teaching of history and social studies. Teachers use this version of the tool to resist teaching from a social justice perspective on two fronts. First, they want to protect the reputation of White people in general from the negative portrayal they receive when topics such as slavery and colonization are exposed. Second, they want to protect White children from learning about these negative acts out of fear that they will feel like "bad people."

Dawn was the only participant who was already a classroom teacher at the time of the interviews, teaching first grade in a predominantly White school. As a result, a great deal of time was spent discussing her approach to the social studies curriculum. She was very concerned about the portrayal of Whites in history and the way this would affect her students' perceptions of themselves. She began, "How can I teach the past and not focus on all the bad things, instead focus on things that are happening now?" In this statement, Dawn has already set up her belief that bad things happened in the past, and things are "more better" now. She continued:

> I mean you have to know about history, but I don't want like all the kids to know that since we are White that we all hurt Black people. So a lot of the books it's about White and White and White did this to the Blacks, so I am trying to figure out ways to stop that so much, and to say the Whites did good for the Blacks and the Blacks did good for the Whites. Not that Whites did bad, Whites did bad, Whites did bad.

Dawn's contradictory statement about the role of history reinforced her problematic understanding that racism was a thing of the past and that progress had changed things. Because Dawn believed that Whites are the true victims of racism, it made no sense to teach a version of history that portrayed Whites as perpetrators of oppression. This was particularly true because she perceived people of Color as using race to receive privileges they do not deserve. Through "Don't bring up the past," Dawn had herself successfully refused to learn about historic racism and was now seeking ways to reproduce her ideology with her own students. Rather than "fix" this problem, the use of this tool allowed her to perpetuate it.

"Protect the Innocent"

Dawn used the tool of "Protect the innocent" to shield her White students from potentially "feeling bad" about themselves when they heard about historical racism.

This perception fit with her sense of being personally attacked when issues of racism were raised, and she was nervous that her students would share this feeling:

> Like when I was talking about Martin Luther King, it was very uncomfortable. Like the kids were like, "Oh, White people are all bad." And I was like, "Nooo! We're not all bad!" And the kids were like, "How come we were bad, and we treated other people badly?" and I was thinking we shouldn't be getting into this and I was getting nervous. ... I don't want them going home and saying we are bad people.

Because Dawn believed that any mention of racism was an attack on all White people, she began to question the appropriateness of teaching about the contributions of Martin Luther King in her classroom. She wanted to protect her students from learning about race because she was unable to imagine a way in which she and her students would not be held personally responsible for racism in the past. Again, since she believed that the system "ain't broke," it particularly did not make sense to risk allowing her students to see themselves as the "bad people" when, in her view, they are actually the victims of racism.

Other participants, Nikki and Laura, took "Don't bring up the past" to a new level when they suggested that multicultural history that addresses racism such as slavery would *cause* students of Color to seek revenge on innocent White people such as themselves. Therefore, to protect all Whites from a possible attack from vengeful students of Color, they believed it best to stay with the traditional curriculum. Nikki claimed:

> Like, I don't know if it's just like that they've only been taught the history where Whites are horrible so that's what sticks in their heads and like that's what gives them some of these images of like when a White person walks into their classrooms. ... I think what a lot of people do is they take this [information about racism], and then some children, well, "revenge" is a strong word, but they want some sort of punishment from it. But it should be more to learn a lesson from it and try to use it in a positive way instead of learning about the ignorance of the past and being mad about it, take that and see what you don't want to do with it and learn a lesson.

Through "Protect the innocent," Nikki wanted to shield Whites from the "punishment" that people of Color might want to carry out on her and other White teachers when they "find out" about racism and historical oppression. In this statement, Nikki reveals her thinking that students of Color as a whole hold negative stereotypes about White people, teachers in particular, and that this is caused by learning about historical racism. Consistent again with the idea that current racism doesn't exist, and that to study it would only make things worse for White people, this tool supports the stance of "It ain't broke" because it justifies the idea that discussing racism is problematic, and in fact is dangerous for White people.

The social justice imperative of equity contends that "special effort must be made to overcome past injustice and inequalities of race, gender and class" (Lipman, 2004, p. 17). The inability or unwillingness of teachers to recognize White privilege or Whiteness as domination through tools such as "Protect the innocent," "Now that things are equal," and "Don't bring up the past" decrease the possibility that they would adopt a social justice stance. These teachers would be unable to support young people to examine multiple forms of oppression because they resist a critique of it themselves. This is a powerful tool, particularly in the hands of teachers, because it provides the rationale for "White-washing" the historical record and dictates what "positive" but inaccurate information will be shared in schools. It negates the need to transform the traditional curriculum and ensures that both students of Color and White students will learn neither the history of racism nor anti-racism in the United States, creating another generation of students who believe "it ain't broke."

Oppositional Stance #2: Hey—Don't Look at Me!

Another oppositional stance, "Hey, don't look at me!" was adopted by the teachers to vehemently refute any connection that they might have to the cycle of racism. As with the "It ain't broke" stance, racism was seen as a thing of the past. Because they "never owned a slave" and were not around in the past, the topic of racism has nothing to do with them. Supported by four Tools of Whiteness, this stance maintained their innocence and belief that racism is not their problem. Aimed at deflecting concepts that connect the participants with racism, such as White privilege, or negating any responsibility for being anti-racist, the "Don't look at me" stance positioned discussions of personal connections to racism as "nit-picky."

"I Never Owned a Slave"

A prevalent tool that upheld the stance of "Don't look at me" was "I never owned a slave." This tool represents the anger and defensiveness that pre-service teachers feel when they are confronted with concepts of racism. Dawn described the anger she experienced when reading about White privilege. "I felt very, very angry because I felt like he [Howard] was trying to make us feel guilty and ... my emotions started to jump in. I felt anger because I never owned a slave ... so why should I be blamed for it now?" The tool of "I never owned a slave" was used here to protect her hegemonic understanding of Whites as victims when challenged with a reading by Gary Howard that suggested that Whites might indeed be the dominant race when looking at societal inequality.

Using this tool served to negate Howard's arguments and the contents of the book, and allowed her to deflect the possibility that she benefited from racism and White privilege. By defensively arguing that she has nothing to do with racism because she never owned a slave (a point that, in fact, Howard never made), Dawn used this tool to discredit *everything* Howard did say about racial identity development and how it impacts teaching that might have helped her to make some connections about how race operates in her own life.

Because the teachers equated any discussion on Whiteness or the role of Whites in history as a personal attack, to discuss slavery was to blame them personally or to try to make them feel guilty. Dawn stated:

> My initial reaction was that I did not hurt or cause pain toward other races and ethnicities. My question was "Why was I part of this theory?" As a person of the White race, I became defensive after reading this section of Howard's book. I feel that I worked hard for everything I gained. No one has given me anything for free or without effort.

The "I never owned a slave" tool functions to dismiss the logic of racism; "You're attacking me, but since I never owned a slave, your ideas about racism aren't making any sense—so don't look at me!" Again, the defensive reaction to the concept of White privilege was not simply resistance. Rather, it was in keeping with her hegemonic story of White victimization and was therefore a Tool of Whiteness aimed at keeping the cycle of racism intact. If teachers are unable to understand the role of race within the history of oppression, they will be unable to support students in examining and challenging racism within their own lives—or taking action against it.

"Stop Making Me Feel Guilty"

Another tool used to deflect racism was "Stop making me feel guilty." Much of the literature on anti-racism (Howard, 1999; Kailin, 1999) explores how part of the process for Whites developing racial consciousness is to experience guilt when they first learn about racism and the role that Whites have played in perpetuating inequality. In contrast, these novice teachers recognized that they were *supposed* to feel guilty and reacted against it by pleading "not guilty." Because feeling guilty would be an admission of responsibility, they explicitly denied this emotion to protect their own innocence in the cycle of racism. Diane, for example, asserted, "Being White is what I was born with. So you know, I'm not going to feel guilty about being White." Upon reflection, she was able to admit to some guilt, but she used another tool, "Everyone's oppressed somehow," to deny the role of race and deflect responsibility:

> I felt like he [Howard] was contradicting himself because he was saying, "I'm not saying you should feel guilty," but every chapter was about like what we did to the Indians or done that to the African Americans, so yeah! It's going to make me feel guilty. But I think that there is always a group that is going to dominate another group of people. You know whether it's Whites over African Americans or Indians over whoever.

Diane's stance of "Hey—don't look at me" allowed her to deflect feeling guilty—or accepting responsibility—by negating the role of race in oppression. She did this by disconnecting Whites from dominance by offering other possibilities of dominant groups (although she could not actually name any other than "whoever"). Not unlike the "I never owned a slave" tool, the "Stop making me feel guilty" tool reinforces the idea that learning about historic racism is an unwarranted personal attack against White people. By using these tools, Whites are able to maintain their construction of personal innocence in the process of racism, destroying the possibility for them to act in racial solidarity with people of Color.

"It's Not Like I Live in a Mansion"

In continuing to justify why racism had nothing to do with them, participants used the tool of "It's not like I live in a mansion." This tool was used to obfuscate differences, helping to maintain a colorblind outlook and to negate disparities. Since, in their view, things really were equal now, why should anyone "look at them" when discussing racism and inequality? Laura, who struggled with the concept of colorblindness, demonstrated how she used the tool with the third-grade class she student-taught in:

> I just wanted to be their friend. I kind of wanted to show them I wasn't bad and I wouldn't mistreat them because they were from a different race, or I had more money or lived in Long Island in a house. We talked about that. [The cooperating teachers said,] "Ms Laura lives in a house, you guys live in an apartment." And they were like, "How many bedrooms you got?" And I was like, "No, my house is small, don't worry." I kind of felt really bad because of the way she was questioning, it was like I lived in a mansion, which I don't. I mean I do have more room. But I turned it around and said, "We all live in different places."

Because of her discomfort with the economic disparities between herself and her students, Laura attempted to diminish these differences when the cooperating teacher mentioned her living conditions. She worried that, because of the class differences between herself and her students, they would hold stereotypes about her and therefore see her as a "bad person" and potentially hold her responsible. She attempted to deny these differences as a way of glossing over race and class inequality. In so doing, Laura used the tool of "It's not like I live in a mansion" as a way of denying inequality, and particularly her role as someone with more advantages.

"Everyone's Oppressed Somehow"

Another Tool of Whiteness used by teachers to support the "Don't look at me" stance is "Everyone's oppressed somehow," which was used to deny the role of race and racism in oppression. The participants repeatedly made statements to deflect the role of race and to claim "everyone is oppressed somehow—not just by the color of their skin." This positioned them as equally oppressed as people of Color, justifying the stance that no one should "look at them" as benefiting from racism. This tool is used by teachers to deny the role of race rather than to complicate it by examining multiple forms of oppression and the intersections of racism with classism, sexism, and homophobia.

One way that the participants enacted the "Don't look at me" stance was to use their religious background, particularly a Jewish identity, as a way to deny the role of race in oppression. This helped them to avoid identifying with the dominant race responsible for racial discrimination. Diane, responding to a reading by Gary Howard about the concept of White privilege, demonstrated this use of the religion:

> Like everybody is judged in some kind of way. Like I've had experiences where I've been judged because I'm Jewish—which has nothing to do with—I mean on the surface I'm White, yes—but I've had people say very negative remarks to me because I'm Jewish. So I feel like he's [Gary Howard] making this a color issue when there is so much more to it than color. I think that made me mad too, because I know that I've experienced that too, and I'm not African American but I've experienced times when—you know.

Diane's identification as a "minority," one who has experienced negative remarks because of her religious affiliation, caused her to reject the idea of racial discrimination, and in particular to deny her identification as a member of the dominant racial group. It was common for the Jewish participants to make what they perceived to be analogous comparisons with anti-Semitism whenever race was brought up. She conceded that she is White, although this is a *surface* identity, as she identifies more strongly as a victim of discrimination as a Jew and is therefore almost more similar to African Americans than to other Whites. This "minority" identification served to shape the teachers' misunderstanding of people of color because, in their minds, if the participants were able to persevere as minorities, why can't everyone? Because "everyone is oppressed somehow," be it by religion or class, then "hey, don't look at" White people, for being at fault for people of Colors' perceived inability to pick themselves up by their bootstraps.

The tool "Everyone's oppressed somehow" conflated racism with other forms of oppression. For example, when asked, Allison could not identify any examples of racism in the schools in which she had student-taught. When asked what that absence made her think of the concepts and content of the course, she replied:

> You can find something wrong with everything, with anything in society. I think that it's like nit-picking. I think there are educational issues, philosophy issues, scientific issues, medical issues. I don't think that there is a true answer because there are soooo many perspectives. You are never going to please everyone.

In her denial of race, she expounded on medical, philosophical, and other issues to create the sense that oppression is "soooo" overwhelming that nothing can be done about it. This alleviated any sense she might have that she should attempt to do something about it. This upheld the problematic assumption that racism is no longer a real issue because there are so many problems in the world and we have no idea if it is race or something else that is a problem—so stop nit-picking.

The Tools of Whiteness that support the "Don't look at me" stance appear at first glance to be resistance to multicultural education. They are consistent, however, with teachers' dominant understandings of the world (racism is over, Whites are victims) and were used to maintain a cycle of racism and White supremacy. The use of these tools directly influence the choices and decisions teachers make, all of which are in opposition to the core concepts of SJE, which call for teachers to explicitly address the institutional inequities that these tools and the "Don't look at me" stance are designed to mask.

Oppositional Stance #3: I Play by the Rules

The "I play by the rules" stance is similar to "Don't look at me" in that they both operate to deflect the taint of racism from the participants' experiences. The difference is that, with "I play by the rules," the participants are willing to acknowledge that racism does negatively impact people of Color. However, by using this stance, the participants believe that, if they follow a set of particular rules that they believe are "not racist," then they are protected from the accusation or benefit of racism or the responsibility of doing anything about it. Rather than reflect upon the role that race and racism plays in their own lives, the use of "I play by the rules" maintains their "innocence" and unwillingness to take action. In addition, it allows them to assign the label *racist* only to overtly racist individuals, such as members of the Ku Klux Klan or Mel Gibson/celebrity racist *du jour* types, further "proving" their own anti-racism.

"I Don't Make Racist Comments"

White people often believe racism is mean words used by thoughtless individuals. When asked to define racism, Kim responded, "I think it's comments. I think it has to be, I mean for comments to even come out, it has to be ingrained in someone's core values and beliefs whether they know it or they don't." Many of the participants shared this understanding of racism as mean-spirited comments. They can, therefore, maintain their position of "I'm not a racist" because they played by the rules—*they* did not make racist comments, had never personally discriminated against anyone, or, as Dawn says, had "never owned a slave." By distancing themselves from racism, they were attempting to remove any sense of responsibility for recognizing ways they might benefit from racial privilege or from having to do anything about racism.

"I Don't Talk about Race"

Remaining silent about issues of race is the purpose of "I don't talk about race," a tool that supports the stance of "I play by the rules." Many White teachers are raised in homes and communities in which race is rarely discussed and have never been in conversations with other people about what it is like to be White. Because of these life experiences, they are reticent and uncomfortable discussing issues of race and believe that, to play by the rules, one shouldn't talk about it. Karen, for example, described how talk about race was silenced in her childhood.

> The whole idea of race was something thought about, like there might have been a joke or a comment, but it was never discussed. It was something you shouldn't say out loud because you never know how someone might take it. So I think that's how you think but you don't say in my family.

Karen explained how she reacted if her family or friends made racist comments, "As long as they are my friends, I would say something. I'm not much of a conflict person, so I'd either ignore them, walk away, and not say anything." Karen initially contended that she would say something, but then she listed three examples of "I don't talk about race," showing what she would be more likely do: "ignore them, walk away, and not say anything." She used this tool she learned in childhood to allow racism to go unchecked in her presence. Because she knew better than to say anything about race "out loud" and acted upon the idea that racism is something that shouldn't be talked about in polite society, she could maintain the stance that she was "playing by the rules" and actually doing a good thing. However, by stifling discussions of race, she is cutting off opportunities to reflect and understand the role that race and privilege have played in her life. If teachers cannot even talk about race, how in the world can they teach about it or fight against racism?

"I Don't Even See Color"

Teachers use the tool of "I don't even see color" to prove their anti-racism and that they play by the rules—if they can't see color, then they cannot discriminate or be racist. Laura in particular struggled with this concept because, on the one hand, she recognized that she did not want to "deny" a child his or her cultural heritage; on the other hand, she saw her recognition of a child's race as an admission that she was stereotyping. This caused her to be very defensive about her stance and to vacillate between wanting to teach from a multicultural perspective while still claiming a certain level of colorblindness:

> I don't go into a classroom and be like "that child is Black, and they're from a shelter, and that child is White, and they're like whatever." But I do know the different races of the children, but that doesn't affect how I will treat any

of those children. … In no way do I want to deny someone his or her culture or skin color. I just do not want to lead anyone to believe that I am prejudiced or a one-sided educator.

By using "I don't even see color," Laura addressed her concern that, by recognizing the race of her students, she would be seen as stereotyping them. Underneath this lay the assumption that only negative aspects are associated with diverse races. This negative association in her mind made her anxious about recognizing race because in her view only inherently negative assumptions would come from such recognition. The real fear of course that was motivating her was of being accused of being racist, rather than the fear of not providing a multicultural education for her students. She was trying to express that she was playing by the rules by treating her students equally, but in her mind equal means the same. In fact, to treat all students the same ensures that she will do no differentiation, culturally relevant teaching, accommodations for English Language Learners, or other strategies that would support a diverse group of students. When enacted, the tool of "I don't even see color" serves to uphold White supremacy by making the creation of culturally relevant or social justice curricula impossible because to do so would recognize diversity, which in Laura's mind was to act on the basis of negative stereotypes.

"I'm Nice to Everyone"

The next rule to play by is to be "nice to everyone," which serves to create an individual response to institutional and societal issues. Many teachers' responses to racism are to rely on adages that have been passed down through their families. This tool invalidates the need for teaching for social justice or taking social action because, as long as they act like nice people, they can maintain their position of innocence in the cycle of racism.

Participants often mentioned their family's philosophies to explain their perspectives on racism. Kim said, "It is something that my dad always taught me, you treat people the way you want to be treated. And it's not that I never felt threatened by anyone, but I just wanted to be a nice person." Even though Kim sees herself as a victim, one who has been threatened, she still plays by the rule of being nice. Other participants also explained that they treat people how they want to be treated, or as Dawn put it, "If you're nice to me, then I'm nice to you."

Nikki explained how she planned to use this tool in her classroom: "But like, you can only do so much … so like just going into the classroom with an open heart and an open mind, and being ready to absorb everything from all these different backgrounds and all these different children—and be able to share yours—that should be enough." Nikki used this tool to negate the need for multicultural preparation when teaching in diverse environments. Since "you can only do so much," it is almost unreasonable to be expected to learn culturally relevant pedagogy, anti-racism practices, English-language acquisition strategies, or any of the other skills being taught in this course because it "should be enough" to have an "open mind." In this way, the tool of "I'm nice to everyone" functioned to uphold White supremacy by perpetuating White teachers' ineffectiveness in urban communities of Color. It maintained White innocence while keeping the focus of urban educational failure on students rather than on their own willful lack of preparation to teach in communities unfamiliar to them.

"I Would Kiss a Black Guy"

The tool of "I would kiss a Black guy" was an extreme expression of the stance of "I play by the rules." An extension of the phrase, "some of my best friends are Black," this tool serves to "prove" that the user is open-minded and therefore anti-racist. Sexualizing racism and anti-racism through the "I would kiss a Black guy" tool is closely linked to the tool of "it's personal not political" because it assumes that personal interactions are a sufficient response to racism and deflects racial privilege and institutional advantages.

Several of the participants raised questions about their lack of friendships with people of Color throughout the course. Amanda, however, took this questioning to an extreme, believing that the ultimate act of anti-racism would be to venture into sexual relations with people of Color, particularly an African American man. In describing to me how she felt some of the other participants in the study were racist, she exclaimed, "Whether they want to put a happy face on it or not. You [classmates] wouldn't date a Black person. You wouldn't! Look at your friends, look at where you are!" In listing characteristics that signified racism, not dating a Black person was an important one to her that she brought up numerous times.

Amanda chose to share a story in which she felt she was "playing by the rules" by being anti-racist in this way. She told me about a party she attended a week earlier at which she had decided, "While I'm here, I'm going to kiss a Black guy! Like that's my goal" because she "just wants to see what it's like to kiss a Black person." During the night she approached an African American man, kissed him, and told him, "It feels the same as kissing a White guy!" When I asked her what she thought might be different, she shared a biological theory she had heard that posited that Blacks and Whites had different smells and even different species assignments.

Of all the participants, Amanda had been the most adamant in her desire to teach African American students. Through course materials and assignments, she had been the most committed to readings and assignments that could better prepare her to work with Black communities, voluntarily reading *The Dreamkeepers* by Gloria Ladson-Billings and articles by Asa Hilliard. Lurking beneath her desire to work with Black children, however, were unquestioned theories about biological racial differences. She concluded her story by stating with pride, "I would not have done it if it weren't for this class. My mind wouldn't have been mind sparked in this way." Through the use of the tool "I would kiss a Black guy," Amanda believed that this interracial sexual "intimacy" was a sign of her growing knowledge and personal action in the area of multicultural education. With a lack of places to turn based on her life experiences, Amanda sought inappropriate avenues to explore her emerging theories about race and difference, and to enact her desire to "play by the rules" by attempting to take what she felt was action against racism.

Oppositional Stance #4: What Do You Expect Me to Do about It?

As the participants' understandings about race ebbed and flowed, some began to recognize the existence of racism. They continued to perceive it as a problem that had nothing to do with them since they played by the rules, and that it only affected people of Color. They continued to hold on to the stance that they did not benefit from racial privilege, but they began to understand that racism did negatively impact others. However, when they felt pressure to potentially do something about such inequities, particularly as future teachers, they adopted the oppositional stance of "What do you expect me to do about it?" Sure, racism existed, but since they were "nice" to others, and "had never owned a slave," what could they possibly be expected to do about it?

This stance was supported by tools that justified their sense of being overwhelmed and disconnected from the magnitude of the problem. The most frequent use of this stance was to diminish the role that one person can have in creating change and therefore relinquish responsibility for taking an anti-racist stance or action as an individual or as a teacher. Comments such as "I'm not going to save the world, you know," "There isn't much I can do," and "How far can one person go?" were commonly stated by the participants as reasons why they remained inactive in the face of racism.

"Out of My Control"

The first tool that supported this stance was "Out of my control," which was used when teachers reflected on multiple societal issues and expressed a feeling of being overwhelmed. Kim used this tool to justify why teacher activism was out of the question for her:

> Currently, I feel no call to become a public racial or ethnic activist. I don't see myself as being in a position where I'm obligated to reform anyone. I can educate, I can learn, but to change another is a task greater than me because we can really only ever take the steps to change ourselves. ... I realize how important it is to address racism if not with others then at least within myself.

Kim believed it to be "out of her control," or not her role as an individual to try to "reform" other people or to take any stance publicly against racism. This use of "Out of my control" fit with her problematic assumptions and use of "it's personal not political," because racism seemed only to be mean comments and individual ignorance. To Kim, as long as she worked on herself, then she would be taking a stance against racism. Justifying this internal anti-racism work as sufficient in and of itself allows social injustice to remain intact because there is no challenge to institutional and societal racism. In this instance, the tool of "Out of my control" was used with another tool, "I'm nice to everyone," which posits that being a good and aware individual is a sufficient anti-racist strategy.

Teachers often use this tool to express frustration when called upon to teach from a social justice perspective. Allison, for example, felt that, "We can work on it in the education aspect, but what happens when the education has to deal with the family and the religious and this and that? It's impossible! You are talking about something that is not possible!" She created the story that, because an individual cannot change everything in society, to expect her to do anything is an unreasonable request—even things that she actually does have control over in her own classroom. She used this tool to justify teaching a traditional, ethnocentric curriculum:

> I kept feeling like that weight on my shoulders, like I'm stepping into a classroom, and if I work in the city it will be multicultural, and he [Howard] kept saying you have to know yourself. Well, that's a lot of pressure in a way! We have enough anxiety as it is going into this classroom, and then, like to tell us "You have to do this, this, this and this, and by the way, you need to be aware of the cultures in your classroom, too." Like I think that makes me even more anxious, upset, and frustrated. And like now I have one more thing to worry about.

Because many teachers like Allison perceive their presence in urban schools to be altruistic and helpful, they are resentful to learn that they might have to do special preparation to work in these under-resourced environments. Allison was indignant that she might be expected to know herself or her students when she was already doing a good deed and was anxious enough about teaching in a "scary" urban school. Because of all the "pressure" she employed "Out of my control," a powerful tool that maintains White supremacy because it justifies inaction on multiple levels.

"I Can't Relate"

Another Tool of Whiteness that backed up "What do you expect me to do about it?" in evidence in the participants' reflections was the tool of "I can't relate." Most of the teachers had no desire to work in "scary" urban schools with students of Color and planned to return to their racially homogenous communities to teach. In order to express this in politically correct terms, they explained that they thought they would be "ineffective" teaching urban students and therefore should "not take jobs in urban schools." Their justification for this was that they claimed it would be difficult to relate to people, particularly students, who were different from themselves and who faced struggles different from their own. In so doing, they released the need to consider that perhaps their aforementioned intense fear of students of Color and urban communities might be the real reason that they did not want to take a position in such schools. This tool allowed them to appear noble, rather than cowardly or racist, in their decision not to teach in urban settings. As Diane demonstrated:

> Well, I was scared that I wasn't going to be able to relate to them. Like unfortunately, they have lived through things that I don't even want to have to imagine and those things I just don't know anything about. And I think it's so important to get to know the child and understand them, so if I don't understand them, or understand where they are coming from, then how am I going to be able to teach them if I can't relate to them?

Diane, who previously had described how "tough" third-grade boys intimidated her, here noted that she was unable to relate to students' "unimaginable" home lives. The differences between her life and the lives of urban students caused her to believe that she could not be expected to teach them, and she continued to rely on assumptions and stereotypes in making career choices. Rather than try to see past her assumptions and stereotypes about students' lives, she took the stance that she couldn't possibly be expected to get to know her students and she therefore washed her hands clean of the whole idea of teaching in a community different than her own. The use of the "I can't relate" tool was consistent with her hegemonic story about fear of difference and people of Color, and the stance that she couldn't be expected to do anything about addressing racism. Clearly in conflict with a social justice stance, this stance allows teachers to walk away from inequality rather than attempt to learn how to address it.

Oppositional Stance #5: Here I Come to Save the Day!

Another oppositional stance, glorified in films such as *Freedom Writers* and *Dangerous Minds*, is that of "Here I come to save the day!" For wealthier Whites, their first relationships with people of Color are often hierarchical in nature. From their nannies and housekeepers to their involvement in charitable activities, the participants positioned themselves as wealthier and higher status, in contrast with people of Color whom they constructed as poorer and needy. Influenced by these early life experiences, the participants continued to see themselves as "good people" for working with people of Color, thus maintaining this hierarchical balance of power in which they were the givers and people of Color were the recipients. The sense that they were good people who could "save" these "poor" children was upheld by the Tools of Whiteness: "I just want to help them."

The "Here I come to save the day!" stance represents a charitable, missionary approach to teaching, which is in direct opposition to a social justice perspective in which teachers see themselves working in solidarity with their students. Rather than questioning or changing conditions that cause structural inequality, the participants worked within a system of oppression without questioning why they themselves were more advantaged by that system than the children they wanted to "save." Working within this paradigm, missionary teachers believe they are doing good, yet they are keeping structures of inequality intact, ensuring that there will always be people in need and others with the resources to "save" them.

"I Just Want to Help Them"

Their childhood sense that they were helping those in need and feeling sorry for students of Color followed the pre-service teachers into their current approaches to teaching. As Laura described her student teaching placement in Harlem:

> And there was one night I had to go home late at night and it was a little scary, and I felt bad being thankful that I don't have to walk through that every night. I think that makes me even more—like I want to help them even more because I have that opportunity. I don't know how that sounds, but I think that's why I wanted that place to connect with those children that I hadn't been around for a long time. I left there so happy.

Because she took a charitable approach rather than a justice orientation to her work at this school, she could feel "happy" about her placement—exercising her good intentions simply by being there. Laura did not look for positive attributes of the community in which she taught and maintained deficit understandings of the people she worked among because she "just wanted to help them." As with the tool of "Out of my control," participants felt like good people and were therefore resentful of having to do additional work to prepare to teach in these communities.

While most of the participants used multiple tools to defend why they did not want to teach in urban public schools, Nikki used the tool of "I just want to help them" to explain why she preferred to teach there. Nikki explained, "I've grown accustomed to it and a lot of what I like is the psychological aspect of it. Like being able to help them cope with their problems." She assigned a "psychological" element to working with public school children that would be absent from working with private school students, where she contended "she wouldn't know their issues or what they are dealing with," despite the fact that she comes from this community:

> I feel like if I'm really devoted to this, I want to help the people who need more help. … I feel better helping everyday public school kids. Where there is, you know, a lot of problems going on in the home, with friends, inside, disabilities affect them. There are just so many problems that like I would want to help fix. Or help be supportive on. In private schools you don't have to deal with that as much.

Nikki assigned a list of deficiencies to "everyday" public school children whom she "feels better helping" because it reaffirmed her identity as a good, charitable person.

Her statement reaffirms her assumption that only public school students are affected by psychological problems or disabilities.

The use of "I just want to help them" raises questions about what specific skills and strategies White teachers like Nikki bring to "fix" these public schools. Because Nikki believed the problems public school children face are based in their homes, a concomitant belief was that love was the only thing needed:

> A lot of these kids in public schools don't get the love and that aspect at home. A lot of the social aspects at home. I am a very open person, I like hug my students and I love them, and I feel like some of them really need to be hugged because they don't get it at home. Some of their parents are like in jail, or their brother is raising them or something while he works like ten other jobs, you know what I mean?

Nikki previously stated that she did not see racism as a current issue, that she did not want to address historical racism in her classroom, and that she resented being asked to do multicultural preparation for this setting. Because she positioned herself as a loving "helper," she would be doing enough simply by being there and providing these "poor children" with the hugs that their incarcerated parents were unable to give them. The idea that urban students of Color are unloved and uncared for is prevalent among White teachers who often view what parenting and love look like through an ethnocentric and classed lens.

The tool of "I just want to help them" maintains the cycle of racism and blocks their development as social justice educators by releasing the need for White teachers to learn skills that address culture and racism in the classroom because they feel they are doing enough by simply going to these communities that "need" their help. Because the perception is that the problems students face are situated solely in their presumably problematic home lives, rather than in institutional racism, there is no need for teachers to examine the ways in which race may be playing a role in students' lives or their own complicity in the cycle of racism. This allows Whites to continue to construct people of Color as deficient and to place the blame of educational failure on communities of Color rather than on the institutions that are inequitably serving them—in direct opposition of the orientation of a social justice educator.

Interrupting the Oppositional Stances and Tools of Whiteness

Collectively, these tools, and the oppositional stances they support, function to block the development of a critical analysis of how racism and oppression operate in education and the larger society. Without these understandings, potential and practicing teachers are able to misrepresent who benefits and who is marginalized by current structures of inequality. The tools allow the teachers to maintain a state of ignorance in which they see no need to create change and they willfully ignore any professional development that might provide them with skills to be more successful in working with students who are different from themselves—which in and of itself maintains inequality. In order to move such teachers along the continuum of development as social justice educators, it is necessary to help interrupt the use of these Tools of Whiteness so that they may begin to gain a stronger political analysis that will in turn allow them to both teach about power and oppression, and gain the skills to transform unjust conditions—the three pillars of SJE.

These stances and tools need to be removed so that teachers can develop two key skills that will allow them to move in the direction of SJE: 1) empathy with people suffering under oppressive circumstances and 2) historical and current knowledge about how inequality operates. To help teachers progress in these areas, I design my courses around constructivist activities that encourage them to build solidarity with people different from themselves and to learn more about oppression and inequality. However, what I have learned that is of critical importance is to create learning experiences in which students "discover" new information or awareness for themselves. If I simply present them with facts about inequality, they quickly filter this information through the Tools of Whiteness in order to maintain their hegemonic understandings. This allows them to not examine or accept new information and they don't move toward SJE. When they have the opportunity, through simulations, role-plays, and other exercises to gain new awareness on their own, they create new knowledge that doesn't get analyzed through their past experiences or tools. This has proven much more effective in helping them to gain empathy and knowledge that moves them toward potentially teaching for justice. In the following section, I share some of the class activities and readings that I use that help students in teacher education courses construct new understandings about inequality and that help them build empathy for people who experience it.

The first oppositional stance, "It ain't broke, so there's nothing to fix," blocks both an understanding that institutional oppression still operates and the fact that the ideology of meritocracy is a fallacy. Removing this block allows teachers to see that the world does not operate on a level playing field. This block needs to be removed so that teachers can understand that their students, families, and communities are not to blame for the conditions in which they find themselves. Additionally, if teachers believe there is nothing to fix, and even further, that Whites are the victims of racism, why would these teachers be motivated to try to create any change that they see as against their best interest? In order to prepare teachers who will challenge actual racial and social injustice, clearly this stance of "there's nothing to fix" must be challenged.

To do so, teachers need to be confronted with the reality that inequality exists and that institutions, systems, and structures work to maintain oppressive conditions that disproportionately impact people of Color. I find that just showing statistics of inequality, i.e. disparities in funding, healthcare, employment, incarceration, etc., does not help as students simply filter them through their Tools of Whiteness, which just reinforces the very stereotypes I'm working to challenge. For example when presented with the disproportionate amount of African Americans in jail or the lower graduation rates of Latinos, rather than see injustice, they say: "Well of course there are more African Americans in jail, they commit more crimes; of course Hispanics have lower graduation rates, their parents don't value education and make their kids work."

What I have found to be more effective is for students to develop empathy by seeing inequality in action. Sharing statistics continues to create distance and "other" people of Color, while empathy helps teachers to try to understand different experiences by putting themselves in other people's shoes. One strategy I use is to show documentaries that chronicle resource inequality in schools, particularly when the films either focus on younger children or are made by young people themselves. Some examples that I have used are: *Children in America's Schools with Bill Moyers* (Hayden, 1996), *Making the Grade* (KQED, 1999), and *The Problem We All Live with* (Fuoco, 2004). These films all do basically the same thing—they follow the experiences of children in both well-resourced and under-resourced schools, highlighting the fact that some children have access and opportunities that, through no fault of their own, others don't. These films do not demonize or "blame" the students in the middle- or high-income schools; they simply portray the differences.

By focusing on individual children's experiences in differently resourced schools, my students begin to see the humanity in these unjust situations. They see and empathize with the people in the film as individual children, rather than thinking about group demographics. Because they begin to identify with the children, they become upset by the unequal circumstances that they face. These films do a good job at helping students see that the United States does not operate as a level playing field and that in fact some children have a head start.

After this notion starts to sink in, I find that this is a better time to start exploring the realities of racism, using readings such as Howard's *We Can't Teach What We Don't Know*, Daniel Tatum's *"Why Are All the Black Kids Sitting Together in the Cafeteria?" And Other Conversations about Race*, and Derman-Sparks' *Teaching/Learning Anti-racism: A Developmental Approach*. These books provide definitions and structural components of racism and share a framework of racial identity development that helps students begin to build a schema about how racism operates.

As a result of these readings, Kim rethought her original understanding of racism as operating only on an individual basis: "I definitely had said something about it [racism] being comments, and now I think: no. That is not just it. I think it can be more than that, it is an institutionalized thing." Laura also began to see previously invisible institutionalized racism in the world around her based on the Derman-Sparks book, "This helped me to take a look at exposing institutionalized racism that includes the mission, policies, organizational structures, and behaviors that are all built into institutional systems and services." After gaining a sense of empathy, Laura not only reworked her original definition of racism from "words hurt" but also to a more complex institutional conception. As a result of gaining empathy and then reviewing comparative situations of inequality, teachers such are these are better positioned as potential social justice educators because they are able to let go of the Tools of Whiteness and begin to see racism for what it is.

Another factor that adds to the "there's nothing to fix" stance is the fact that many of my students are missing the historical background knowledge needed to understand how racism and other forms of oppression have come to be. Without this information, it is challenging for them to see institutional racism, as they see racism as just random acts of meanness. They also find it difficult to not blame people of Color for their circumstances because they do not have an understanding of how historical oppression has created unequal contexts. Books like Spring's *Deculturalization and the Struggle for Equality*, Loewen's *Lies My Teacher Told Me*, and Zinn's *A People's History of the United States* all help students to see that these forces have been at work for a long time—racism isn't something that happened in the 1950s that Martin Luther King and Ruby Bridges ended. These readings often create a sense of cognitive dissonance between what is in the book and what my students previously learned in school. This dissonance can be capitalized on to help them construct new knowledge and to see that, indeed, something needs to be fixed.

By learning a new, more complex understanding of the way textbooks present history from grade level to grade level, Dawn experienced a dramatic disruption in her belief system through reading *Lies My Teacher Told Me*. She lamented to the textbook companies who left information out of her books: "Why didn't you tell me this? It leaves me looking like a total idiot! ... What happened to the 'friendly' pilgrims? Why didn't anyone tell me about the plague that murdered the Native Americans?" Before reading this book, Dawn had used her oppositional stances to remain preoccupied for much of the course with teaching "positive" stories of US history. Through her exposure to readings that gave her a historical background knowledge that caused cognitive dissonance with her own education, she became aware of the holes in her own knowledge and how that influenced her hegemonic understandings.

Despite articulating the most ardent hegemonic understandings, and being the most prolific user of the Tools of Whiteness, this reading transformed Dawn's thinking about history, racism, and the way in which she planned to teach about it. This transformation better enabled her to teach from a social justice perspective because, rather than trying to dismiss social studies that address oppression, she planned to transform her own curriculum:

> While teaching the first Thanksgiving to my first graders this year, I left out important details, which fully change the meaning of the event. This year my main goal ... was, including what the Pilgrims and Indians wore, ate, and did on this festive day. Next year ... I would like the children to be able to see the real relationship between the pilgrims and the smaller group of Indians to learn how the Pilgrims really settled onto the Native American lands.

By removing the blinders of the existence of oppression, this reading and some of the activities we did with it transformed her teaching from a traditional heroes and holidays approach in which the main objectives were focused on food and clothing, to a lesson that addressed a more accurate depiction of European colonization.

When students are able to put down their tools so that they can interpret new knowledge, students like Dawn often are able to put aside their oppositional stance of "It ain't broke" and come around to the idea that something "needs to be fixed." The next stance, "Don't look at me," however, is a tougher nut to crack. While more challenging, it can be accomplished by getting teachers to recognize that they too are implicated in this system of inequality. It is one thing for them to admit that other people have it hard, but it's another to recognize that they have had it "easy," or at least easier given the role that patriarchy, class, and other forms of oppression play in people's lived experiences.

The "Don't look at me" oppositional stance functions to refute teachers' connection to, or their role in, the cycle of racism. If teachers believe that "racism is something that hurts others, but it doesn't help me," they may be motivated to do something about inequality, but what they come up with will be based in sympathy and charity (such as a food or penny drive) rather than solidarity and justice. To help transform this understanding, it is necessary to help White pre-service teachers see that racism is maintained by a system that oppresses some while simultaneously benefitting others—namely themselves. I do this through a constructivist activity that forces them to acknowledge that privilege exists before they have the chance to use their Tools of Whiteness.

Like the truism that you don't know what you don't know, White people often don't know how much they benefit from racism. This causes a great deal of defensiveness and denial when the idea of White privilege is introduced. As a way into challenging this oppositional stance, I usually start with a simulation activity adopted from Lawrence (1998) that illuminates how inequality and privilege operates.

Students are divided into about four groups and each group is told they will be given art materials to create a visual representation of their understanding of social justice. The groups are given some time to start planning and then they are given bags of arts and crafts supplies. Unbeknownst to them, I have prepared the bags to have disparate amounts of materials; the "privileged" group has an abundance of scissors, papers, glitter, glue, etc. The "under-resourced" groups are provided with one or two crumpled post-its, a dried glue stick, some highlighters, etc. The two other groups are given supplies somewhere in the middle. As the groups try to create what they had envisioned, I walk around and provide warm, constructive, and enthusiastic feedback to the privileged group and short, cold directives ("Please pick the scraps off the floor") to the under-resourced group. I completely ignore the middle-resourced groups.

Invariably, the same response unfolds every time I do this activity. The students with all of the resources are laughing, joking, and enjoying their time to create their representation. They focus on each other and the task at hand, completely oblivious to what is happening in the rest of the room. The students in the under-resourced group look dejectedly at their materials, look to me for a reaction, and, when they receive none, start to complain to each other about what they have. Almost immediately, they start looking around to compare what they have with what the other groups have received. After a few minutes of this, sometimes making loud comments about their materials, they set to work to create something with what they have. After about 15 minutes, the students complete their representations and each group presents their projects. It is not until the group with the least amount of materials presents, usually apologetically, that the class begins to realize that there was something deeper going on in this simulation.

While the debriefing of this activity brings many issues to the forefront, one new awareness is particularly powerful in breaking down the "Don't look at me" stance. In the debrief, the privileged group has to acknowledge that they were *unaware* of the unequal distribution of resources because they had everything they needed (as did most of the middle groups). Because the students experienced and named this phenomenon themselves, it lays an important foundation that I can return to when the students subsequently try to use their tools to deny White privilege—that when you have privilege you often don't even realize it exists. This supports students in starting to loosen their grip on the idea that there are people who are both advantaged and disadvantaged by racism, and it serves as an experiential introduction to readings and activities on White privilege such as McIntosh's *Unpacking the Invisible Knapsack* in which the author recounts all the White privileges she receives in her daily life.

In an attempt to continue to remove the block of "Don't look at me," I borrow a writing assignment from Julie Kailin's *Antiracist Education*, and have students write a "racial autobiography" about their life in which they recount their experiences with people who are different from themselves during significant periods of time in their life. This helps the students think about the messages they have received about race and difference throughout their socialization, and to make decisions now about which of these previously unexamined ideas they want to hold on to, and which they are willing to let go. It helps my White students realize that they too have a racial identity. (Or as Dawn put it, "before [this assignment] I never realized that I was actually considered a race type thing. I just see things differently now.") Rather than me as the instructor recite the different ways that people experience race and racism, this assignment provides students with the opportunity to explore the role that race has played in their own lives. Because they make the connections themselves, they are less likely to use their Tools of Whiteness to try to fight me.

By doing the privilege game prior to the writing assignment, students are more willing to name uncomfortable memories that show the role that race has played in organizing their life to benefit them in certain ways—i.e. hierarchical relationships with people of Color, access to honors or AP classes, being shielded from large class sizes or detention or other experiences that their peers of Color might have dealt with. As Allison testified, "I have never learned as much about myself than in writing the multicultural autobiography. ... I haven't stopped wondering about ... my experience as a child with live-in help and housekeeping." Allison began to look more deeply at the power relations and hierarchy involved in her previously unexamined perception that her live-in "help" were equal members of her family. By being able to understand how race has shaped their own lives, White teachers like Allison are in a better position to set aside their oppositional stances and think more realistically about the nature of difference and inequality.

These activities and assignments also allowed Allison to begin to wonder about other ways that White privilege shaped her life. In her reflective writings, she reflected on a promotion she had been chosen for over her West Indian colleagues. In her autobiography, she reflected that perhaps White privilege had played a role in this, stating, "I think you don't realize it until you look back at it and it's shown to you. I just thought, 'right out of college, got the job, this is great' and now I'm like, 'hmmm, that [White privilege] could be it.'" Providing my students with opportunities to examine how White privilege plays out in their own lives helps them to recognize its existence. This kind of critical self-awareness is a key component in the ability to work in solidarity with communities of Color. As teachers, Whites who self-reflect and own their racial privilege are better positioned to start teaching about racism because they will begin to have an analysis that examines structural oppression rather than seeing people of Color as victims and Whites as innocents.

The next oppositional stance, "I play by the rules," and supporting tools such as "I don't even see color" caused the students to believe that it is racist to recognize color. This is a stance antithetical to SJE because it stifles teachers from being able to actually get to know who their students are and where they come from. Therefore this stance blocks their ability to develop culturally relevant curriculum based upon their students' interests and experiences.

Some of the course readings by authors such as Nieto, Delpit, Ladson-Billings, Hilliard, Chang and Au, and Kailin are aimed at challenging the notion of color-blindness and encourage teachers to recognize and build upon the diversity in their classrooms. I found early on that my students relied heavily on their Tools of Whiteness when doing these readings. Rather than carefully reading for understanding, the students would find one thing to disagree with based on their hegemonic understandings and use that as an opportunity to dismiss the whole thing without trying to understand the authors' perspectives.

To counter this, I adapted a "talk show" activity that I previously used in my elementary classroom designed to help students understand different characters' motivations and perspectives. The new activity is a combination of a role-play and a traditional "jigsaw" in which students split up different articles and then share their article with people who read other papers so that everyone walks away with some information from all articles. In my version, the students are split into author groups (usually some combination of the authors named above) and they have to present the material in the article *as the author* on a talk show. I personally enjoy making it *The Oprah Show* because everyone is familiar with it and it is easy to "ham it up," which makes the students more relaxed and engaged. (A male colleague of mine does *The Montel Show*.) With Oprah off the air, this might have to change in the coming years.

Given the questions in advance for homework, the students have time in their author-alike groups to be sure they really understand the material and can present it in role. When the talk-show portion begins, I really play it up as "Oprah" and welcome everyone to my studio. I start by asking a question to one author, and a member of that group comes "on stage" with a placard around her neck with the author's name. As this "author" presents "her" work, the other audience has to listen for connections to their own reading. For example, a student as Lisa Delpit may start talking about the dangers of stereotyping students and may share an example from the reading of a teacher who stereotyped an Asian American student as being good at math, when in fact the child needed support. A student who read an article by Benji Chang and Wayne Au may hear a connection and then take her placard, come to the stage and add to the conversation by sharing the thesis of her reading that aims to dismantle the myth of Asians as the "model" minority.

This talk show activity forces the students first and foremost to understand the authors' perspectives rather than to immediately discredit the information by filtering it through the Tools of Whiteness. Through this activity, my students gain new information and change their thinking about the value of ignoring racial difference. Dawn stated:

> I used to be one of those teachers who did not see color. I thought if I ignored differences, I would be able to form a closer classroom community. After reading Sonia Nieto, I learned that looking at all of my students the same way was actually hurting them. Nieto taught me that connecting curriculum to students' lives and identities helps them to succeed in the classroom and in daily life. In the classroom, I now give students the opportunity to reflect on their culture, race, and family life during daily lessons.

By laying down the "I don't even see color" tool, Dawn transformed both her thinking and her practice based on a careful reading of what the author was actually saying that challenged her original thought that it is best to ignore differences. This enabled her to change her thinking in ways more aligned with SJE. She reflected:

> In the long run, I realized that I was actually hurting them [my students] ... I was teaching that everyone needs to be blond, blue-eyed, skinny type thing. I wasn't doing it purposely, but it just came out that way, and I was just kind of denying that.

In addition to now *seeing* race, laying down the Tools of Whiteness allowed the teachers to speak about racial difference in ways that they originally did not.

Part of the next oppositional stance, "What do you expect me to do about it?" posits that, sure, maybe racism exists, but doing something about it is outside of these teachers' responsibility. The use of the "I can't relate" Tool of Whiteness supports this stance when teachers believe their lives are so different than the assumed abysmal lives of their students that it would be impossible to effectively teach them. This stance is often rooted in a complete lack of empathy for people who live lives different from themselves.

Without putting down this tool, teachers see their students and their lives only as a laundry list of problems, making them unable to look past students' more challenging behavior, and making meaningful and reciprocal relationships impossible. Unable to connect to students, the teachers' efforts at classroom management and instruction fail, and they in turn blame their students for what has ultimately stemmed from their own negative and stereotyped views of their students. Until this pattern is addressed, SJE is an impossible hope for such teachers.

As a strategy to address this, I created the Child Connection Assignment as an attempt to help move my students away from deficit thinking toward becoming advocates for the children in their student teaching placements. My student-teachers begin by identifying a child with whom they struggled to connect. Each student-teacher then observes this child and writes up an observation as well as an "empathy journal" in which the student-teacher writes from the child's perspective in order to try to imagine how the child is experiencing the classroom. Before turning these assignments in, the class examines an actual write-up from a former student-teacher that is riddled with deficit descriptions of a child who is presented as nothing but a list of problems. The current student-teachers identify examples of "deficit" thinking, a term that is introduced in class through the use of a reading by Lois Weiner. They return to their own write-up, identifying their own moments of deficit thinking, and reframe these sentences to present their students in less judgmental terms. For example, candidates may reframe "Darnell is uninterested in learning" to "During read-aloud, when most students are looking at the teacher, Darnell is playing with his shoelaces."

By focusing on the child rather than a label, my students begin to move away from making sweeping assumptions about the children they work with. After reflecting on what they notice about themselves and how they observe children, my students work on developing a personal connection with their assignment student. They have to engage in a conversation in which they demonstrate to the child that they are thinking about them as a whole person—for example, noticing the child's love of Spider-Man and bringing a print-out from the web about the most recent movie. My students reflect on this conversation and how it shifts their relationship with the child.

Finally, they write letters to the child's future teacher, advocating for the student and identifying strategies that could help this student in their future classroom. By moving from seeing only deficits to recognizing the whole child and their strengths, teachers are in a better position to be able to develop solidarity with this child. This assignment helps them to recognize the potentially dangerous conceptualizations they may hold about their students and explicitly helps them to reframe their stance to that of solidarity and advocacy.

For many students, this assignment becomes a transformative experience that facilitates their transition from the role of watchdog to advocate. After this experience, my students express a desire to better understand who their students are and where they come from, and there was evidence they developed strategies to better meet these goals. For example, Diane initially struggled to get to know her case study student, an African American third grader named Keisha whom she defined solely by her "issues": "she had issues with the lunchroom teacher, she had issues with the other teachers, she had issues with the Para [the paraprofessional], she'd had issues with like everybody, and really I think that she has issues in general."

Diane initially saw Keisha as simply a list of "issues." As part of the case study, Diane was asked to engage Keisha in conversations about her interests and to learn more about her as an individual and as a student. Diane described a "breakthrough" in their relationship as Keisha began to confide in her and tell her about the challenges she faced. Diane learned that Keisha was in foster care and that she rarely was able to see her mother. Diane stated:

> That kind of made more sense to me why she was so standoffish with me at first, you know, like because she's been bumped from here to there, whatever, she's not going to just warm up to everybody, you know? So after I started to work with her more and, you know, by like talking about the books and things like that and bringing in things that she liked, I started to get to know her more. It's easier for me to relate to her and understand where she was coming from.

Diane articulated the importance of getting to know Keisha and familiarizing herself with Keisha's life circumstances so Diane could learn how they were affecting her classroom behaviors. Diane's approach changed from listing her "issues" to developing empathy for what Keisha was facing, and she was able to name the actions she took that helped to strengthen their relationship. She even claimed, in a monumental transformation for Diane, that she could "*relate*" to her.

Of all the participants, Diane had been the most unwavering in her repeated ideology that she couldn't relate to or teach children who didn't share her background. After this assignment, she expounded on the importance of getting to know students, claiming that "now I think that it's important to take that extra effort and get to know kids and, you know, work with them one on one and get to know them on that personal level." Diane's attitude toward children different from herself was transformed as she learned the skills of getting to know children as individuals. Her initial hegemonic understanding of her third graders as "tough" and "scary" became one in which she spoke with empathy about students' lives. This shift is one that better positions Diane to teach from a perspective of social justice, if she so chooses.

The final oppositional stance discussed is "Here I come to save the day!" with the corresponding Tool of Whiteness, "I just want to help them." At this stage, teachers recognize racism, they know that it is wrong, and they want to do something about it. These are all good things and are necessary mindsets in order to be an educator for justice. However, by using "Here I come to save the day!" teachers construct themselves as superheroes who will swoop in and save "these poor kids" from their families and communities who are perceived to not care about their children. With this stance, teachers do not act in solidarity with communities of Color against a system of oppression; rather they continue to perceive communities of Color as the problem from which their students need saving. For new, young White teachers, this is an important stance to tackle because it is one that is glorified and perpetuated by the mainstream media.

The first step in helping my students release the stance of "Here I come to save the day!" is to help them recognize it when they see it. I do this by leading them in a critical media literacy activity using the popular Hollywood film, *Freedom Writers*. This film paints a picture of Erin, a new, naïve, White teacher who begins teaching in the crime-infested, gang-ridden, tough, and dangerous schools of East Palo Alto. Erin, who receives no support from other teachers, administrators, parents, and her own family, sacrifices her time, money, personal relationships, even her marriage, to "save" her students, all of whom are portrayed as coming from "broken" homes. Based on a true story, the exercise I do is not to indict the real-life teacher, Erin Gruwell, but rather to help my students to begin to recognize the popular narrative of the White savior who is single-handedly able to help gang-affili-ated, drug-selling, illiterate students of Color who come from homes infested with guns, domestic-violence, prostitution, and drugs.

My goal is to help my students deconstruct what the director wants us to believe about this story based on the information the film chooses to share with us. This is so they can see this as representing a certain perspective, and for them to think about the messages they are receiving as new teachers. Because it is a well-made film with quality actors and because the messages fit my students' ideology, it is hard for my students not to identify with Erin and what she is going through. To try to break through this challenge, I find it helpful to use language like "how does the film portray" rather than focus on individual characters and their actions.

I pair my students up, each pair consisting of an "A" partner and a "B" partner. They are given a worksheet to jot down observations in boxes as they watch the film. The "A"s jot down how the film portrays: 1) communities of Color, 2) urban schools, and 3) students of Color and their parents. The "B"s take notes on how the film portrays: 1) White teachers, 2) experienced teachers and administrators, and 3) successful instructional strategies and content curriculum. I stop the film at strategic points to allow the "A"s and "B"s to share their notes with each other and have a few whole-class comments.

Through this process, students are able to identify the portrayal of Erin as the savior and the one-dimensional deficit-oriented depiction of the students and their communities. They are also able to pick up on some of the more subtle messages that they feel they are supposed to internalize as new teachers. They name that they feel they are being told that, as new teachers, they can expect to be the only people who will care about their students and that there will be no place they can turn to for support. This message is an important one to challenge because going into teaching with a lone-stallion approach would cut these teachers off from communities of support and particularly from veteran teachers of Color who could teach them about this new environment. Social justice educators see themselves as part of communities acting in solidarity, so it is helpful that they are able to name how the film undermines this idea. I usually end the activity showing a spoof of the film from MadTV called *Nice White Lady* that is a comical yet biting satire of the themes of race in urban education.

Because *Freedom Writers* is so compelling, and most of my students have already seen it, this exercise has proven effective at helping them break down the messages that the popular media perpetuates about teaching. One semester during this exercise, a Dominican American student turned to me, with tears in her eyes, and explained that this film had originally motivated her to become a teacher. She shared her hurt with me upon realizing that she hadn't noticed what they were saying about people like her and similar communities; she had only identified with the teacher. This moment highlights that all people are targets for internalizing racist ideology, not just White students, and activities such as this are important for all teachers to learn to deconstruct the sources of many hegemonic understandings. Of course, watching and discussing one film is hardly sufficient in destroying the "Here I come to save the day!" attitude that inspired many teachers to enter the profession, but being able to recognize it is an important first step.

Conclusion

In concert with each other, the oppositional stances and Tools of Whiteness function to uphold teachers' problematic assumptions concerning race and difference. The women in this study called upon these tools as response mechanisms when their understandings of the world were challenged. They were able to dismiss racism, negate responsibility, reverse the role of oppressors and the oppressed, and justify inaction on issues of race. While often analyzed as resistance, these Tools of Whiteness are instead a proactive protection of hegemony and White supremacy, and serve as serious barriers to a vision of SJE in which teachers work for justice both inside and outside of the classroom.

Teacher activism requires that teachers have a political analysis of oppression and a drive to do something about it. The Tools of Whiteness kept the teachers in this chapter from developing a critical awareness of race or even a willingness to recognize the existence of inequality, guaranteeing that they will not move toward activism. Teacher education can play a role in helping to interrupt the Tools of Whiteness that can provide pre-service teachers with some of the requisite qualities of teaching for justice. By engaging students in activities in which they have to "discover" new information or come to their own conclusions about injustice, students are able to develop new understandings unfiltered by the Tools of Whiteness.

While one semester of multicultural education is insufficient to counteract a lifetime of hegemonic understandings, teacher education must see one of its central roles as helping pre-service candidates reverse their oppositional stances and lay down their Tools of Whiteness. If this can be accomplished, new teachers will be better positioned to teach for social justice because they will at the very least begin to develop a political analysis of oppression. Gaining these new understandings certainly does not guarantee that pre-service teachers will commit to SJE, but it at least puts them in a position where they can make an informed choice about what kind of teacher they would like to be. Without that foundation, teaching about injustice or taking action against it are pipe dreams.

Moving pre-service teachers away from using these tools is one role of teacher education for social justice. However, an even more powerful role is recruiting teachers who don't use these tools in the first place. Some argue that the urgency for teachers who can best serve students of Color is so great that teacher education should move away from working to transform White teachers' belief system and move to finding innovative ways to recruit more teachers of Color into the profession (Sleeter, 2001). Programs such as "Grow your own" in Chicago are starting up across the country as an attempt to prepare community members to become teachers in neighborhood schools. Finding ways to prepare parents, paraprofessionals, and students from "hard to staff" communities as teachers has become the focus of several teacher education programs (Villegas, 2008). Finding teachers from within such communities who believe in the capacity and strengths of their students is one potential way to bring teachers to the field who already understand what students face and may be more willing to work for justice.

As more traditional schools of education are likely to continue to accept vast numbers of pre-service teachers from communities different from where they will teach, teacher education has a critical responsibility to continue to move all educators toward SJE. Fortunately for those of us concerned with social justice, not all teachers who have been socialized to have hegemonic understandings about race and difference use the Tools of Whiteness when their beliefs are challenged. In fact, many choose to reject the tools and instead begin to actively question their belief system and recognize the "matrix" of White supremacy to which they had previously been blind. The next chapter turns to a group of such teachers and examines the ways in which they worked to implement their developing sense of justice into their classrooms.

3

TEACHING FOR JUSTICE

Developing Strategies for Integrating SJE in the Classroom

While the last chapter focused on teachers who used the Tools of Whiteness to avoid having to recognize inequality, power, or privilege, this chapter examines new, young teachers who, in contrast, developed an emerging sense of social injustice. The teachers in the last chapter were unwilling to take responsibility for their own racial privilege and saw no reason to take action for social justice. In contrast, the emerging social justice teachers, who were also former students of mine, had a budding interest in inequality and wanted to become the kinds of teachers who would address social issues in their classrooms. Unlike the teachers in the last chapter, these emerging social justice educators were willing to seek out a space in which to grow and transform. They joined a Social Justice Critical Inquiry Project (CIP) that I facilitated so that they could reach their goal of integrating social issues into the classroom.

After working with the graduate students featured in Chapter 2, I taught a cohort of undergraduate pre-service teachers for two years, also focusing on issues of social justice. Working with these two different groups of pre-service teachers was like night and day. Instead of spending my time figuring out how to combat the Tools of Whiteness, many of my undergraduate students were open-minded and excited about the potential of creating transformative classroom spaces where students grappled with real-world issues. Their excitement was contagious and I wanted to be able to support those that were going straight into teaching in New York City after they graduated.

To provide this support, I created CIP so they could work with myself and their peers to continue to develop as social justice educators. Based on work by Duncan-Andrade (2005) and my own subsequent pilot version of such a group (Picower, 2007), critical inquiry groups provide a space for teachers to examine their own practice. The social justice critical inquiry group that I facilitated and that is written about in the next two chapters ended up being a five-year project with new alumni from my courses joining after graduation every year. This chapter is based on the first year of the group.

The major differences between the teachers in the second chapter and what the CIPers brought to the table were that CIPers felt a "sense of injustice" when they learned about issues of inequality. I use the phrase "sense of injustice" deliberately. In contrast to a drive, a calling, or a passion, a "sense" of injustice points to the emerging nature of their understanding of inequality. They had an understanding that injustice was wrong and a sense of empathy for people whose lives had been caused pain by oppression. While this sense of injustice motivated them to want to learn more about issues such as racism and poverty, it still had nebulous qualities pointing to the amount that they still had to learn in order to have a complex political analysis of how inequality operates. However, they were absolutely clear that they wanted to develop curriculum to teach about social issues and they saw this as a form of activism. While Chapter 4 will discuss the ways in which teaching about injustice is an incomplete strategy for change, this chapter will examine the creative ways that these teachers managed to reach their goal of teaching about social justice in settings that were not always friendly to such curricula.

The emerging social justice educators in this chapter may have had a desire to teach social issues, but they faced a number of barriers in trying to reach their goals. Like other new educators concerned with social justice, they faced a daunting task as they began teaching in the neoliberal context of American schooling. In addition to learning how to teach, these new educators had to negotiate challenges such as mandated curriculum, high-stakes testing, and colleagues who didn't share their political ideology. This environment created a state of fear for these new teachers as they found themselves alienated in a system where it was unclear whom to turn to for support.

By developing four survival strategies, these emerging teachers were able to reach their goal of integrating social issues into their classroom curricula. First, these teachers worked together to build a safe haven that supported their pedagogical efforts while defending themselves from criticism from within their individual school contexts. Second, the teachers camouflaged their social justice pedagogy within their classrooms by using tactics such as integrating it with the mandated curriculum or substituting alternative materials. Third, the teachers prepared their students to become critically conscious of larger systems of inequity and taught them the tools they will need to struggle for social change. Fourth, in a few instances, the teachers went public with their stances by openly rejecting school policies and publicly voicing their dissent. By using these strategies, the teachers were successful in creating classrooms where students engaged in critical social justice pedagogy.

The first year of CIP began with a one-day retreat and then regular biweekly dinner meetings were held in the fall with six teachers.[1] Early meetings were dedicated to developing shared norms, goals, and future agendas. The meetings consisted of focused discussions on shared readings, curriculum development, lesson feedback, presentation preparation, and general issues and concerns that arose from their classroom settings. Of the teachers, four were White, one was African American, and one was Latina. Four of the six participants were full-time classroom teachers. The two other participants were still taking education classes. I served as both the facilitator and researcher of the group. This chapter is based on data collected during this first year. The group grew and new members joined in each of the subsequent four years of the project.

Teaching in a State of Fear

The school environments that many educators, such as the ones in CIP, find themselves within make it difficult to teach for social justice inside the classroom. By allowing policy makers inexperienced in education to use corporate trends, rather than community voices, to decide what curricular packages should be used in schools (Kozol, 2007; Privatization of Public Schools, 2008) and by relying on high-stakes testing and merit pay as tools for accountability (Sleeter, 2007), such policy makers control what information and ideological perspectives are shared in schools. This outside control serves to reproduce inequality rather than create environments that engage students in struggles against oppression. Therefore, much of the neoliberal agenda that dictates local and school policy creates a "state of fear" for educators who wish to veer from this corporate-driven status quo of teaching as usual. For teachers who explicitly want to provide a different kind of educational experience for their students, this state of fear severely limits their ability to teach for social justice because of the constant monitoring and policing of their classrooms and curriculum. This state of fear refers both to the emotional state that individual educators find themselves in, as well as the general environment of schools in which teachers and administrators find their jobs and autonomy threatened if they do not conform to the pressures of school accountability policies.

Because the CIP members wanted to teach about issues that veered from mainstream ideology, the implementation of these policies at the local level created a politically charged terrain that was difficult to navigate. This state of fear was reinforced by colleagues and administrators who, under the same pressures to conform to normative styles of education, functioned as spies and traitors because of their inability or unwillingness to take risks to transform their own classrooms. This made it challenging for the CIP teachers to know who to trust or with whom they could collaborate. From ideologically intimidating teacher lounges to testing policies and curricular mandates, their school climate was filled with landmines that made it difficult to feel safe or to learn how to use their classrooms for social change.

The maintenance of this state of fear requires strict control over what information is taught and what political ideology is reproduced in schools. As Bowles and Gintis (1976) explained, "dominant classes seeking a stable social order have consistently nurtured and underwritten these ideological facades and, insofar as their power permitted, blocked the emergence of alternatives" (p. 104). To this end, two current tools used to reproduce the status quo in schools are mandated curricula and standardized testing (Oakes & Lipton, 2007; Sleeter, 2005). Mandated curriculum can take the form of a textbook, a loosely defined program, or a tightly controlled curriculum supervised by coaches or administrators who strictly monitor the way in which the program is delivered. These function as tools of the neoliberal state in that they funnel public funding to private corporations and are framed as strategies that ostensibly help support student learning (Kumashiro, 2008). In reality, they function to carefully control and monitor the content, form, and ideological perspective of the instruction that students receive, while requiring constant monitoring and surveillance to ensure conformity.

While many educators surrender to these forms of oversight and control, the CIP members began to recognize the dilemma teachers face and the way in which resisting the mandated curriculum was a political choice they needed to make. Jonathan, a fifth-grade special education teacher, learned to recognize the inherently political nature of curriculum and that to obediently follow the mandated curriculum is not neutral, but rather is to side with the status quo. Developing this awareness was critical to Jonathan and the other CIPers' understanding that teaching for social justice requires taking risks and making waves in a sea of conformity. Jonathan reflected, "One of the understandings I've been coming to over the last four years is that this [SJE] is not neutral. There is a lot of fear that am I going to offend someone, or that I am going to get fired for this. But it's really about knowing what your opinion is and choosing a side." Jonathan recognized that there are potential consequences and risks associated with social justice education and that teachers must take an active stand. He continued, "It's [SJE] a very active process, you can't be passive. It's more than just communicating information … and that is a big part about whether you are a social justice educator or just doing what another history book says." Unlike the teachers in Chapter 2, CIP teachers understood the political nature of teaching and were willing to take risks, key characteristics of social justice educators.

For Jonathan and Stephanie, also a public school fifth-grade teacher, one of the most restrictive policies of the neoliberal context was the mandated literacy curriculum, the Teachers College Reading and Writing Project (TC). The TC program, adopted citywide in 2003 under New York City's Mayoral Control, was an attempt to standardize curriculum across schools (Traub, 2003). While the program pedagogically has both advantages and challenges, the blanket way that it has been enforced in city schools has served to negate teacher autonomy and ignores local context. Each school has a literacy coach on staff, and has regular visits from TC consultants who train the teachers to identically implement the curriculum across classrooms and schools. Jonathan explained,

> The reading and writing curriculum is kind of dull, and social studies keeps getting pushed off to the side, especially in NYC public schools. At the elementary school level, it's either not taught or it's something boring like

> map skills or latitude and longitude. ... Unfortunately in NYC public
> schools, the curriculum is really rigid.

As Jonathan articulates, social studies, the subject most amenable to social justice, had virtually disappeared from the curriculum because of the national emphasis on reading test scores. A national survey on the effects of No Child Left Behind showed that 71 percent of school districts reduced instructional time in subjects other than math and reading, with social studies reported as the most frequently cut subject area (Westheimer & Kahne, 2007). As a group, the CIP teachers repeatedly expressed concern about their students' lack of historical knowledge ("How does a fifth grader not know what 9/11 is?") and this became a driving motivation for their pursuit of developing strategies to address social issues in their classrooms.

By making it difficult, if not impossible, for teachers to provide social studies instruction, the use of mandated curriculum is producing a generation of students who are not learning about where they come from or why current inequalities exist. The strategy of stealing the history of oppressed people can result in internalized feelings of inferiority or blame for their circumstances created not by personal failure but by institutionalized oppression (Freire, 1970; Loewen, 1996). This is one of the most problematic effects of federal policies and how they play out in local contexts.

CIP teachers also recognized their own lack of historical knowledge as a detriment to teaching social studies. Demonstrating another difference with the teachers in Chapter 2, these teachers tried to fill in some of their perceived gaps. As Amanda from Chapter 2 expressed, "Like I had been taught that Columbus discovered America, and then somewhere along the way I had heard that he didn't, but I never looked into it. Because it's something I just don't care about." In contrast, the CIP group dedicated several sessions to educating themselves on historical knowledge they felt they were lacking background in, such as Malcolm X and immigration issues. This growing historical content knowledge helped them to better integrate issues of social justice into their curriculum.

The rigidity of the curriculum the CIP members were given and the pressure to conform to it was confounded by the high-stakes testing environment of NYC schools. As fifth-grade teachers, Jonathan and Stephanie shared that they were responsible for administering dozens of standardized tests over the course of the year. Jonathan explained that, from December to March, the entire school's focus is only on preparing students for the tests. Stephanie clearly understood the broader political and economic context that drove the test prep frenzy in her school. "They're spending money for me to go to a test prep PD [professional development] to learn how to do this garbage and how to teach garbage better when they could be sending me to a PD where I could learn how to create a thematic unit with great social justice themes." Stephanie, like others in the group, was infuriated that her school was prioritizing testing, a policy that she saw as harmful to her students, over programs that she believed could better prepare her to lead her students to be successful and engaged citizens.

As an emerging social justice educator teaching in a neoliberal context, Stephanie was beginning to develop a political analysis of the forces and pressures that determined the kind of professional development she received. She continued:

> So why are they sending me here and not there? Because tests are the most important thing to administrators because the most important thing is the school report card, and if it isn't up to par, that means test scores aren't up to par, which means THEY aren't up to par. So they have to make sure that the teachers are teaching to the test because if not it makes them look bad. And, you know all those principals want that $25,000 bonus they get if they get an 'A' [emphasis in original].

Stephanie recognized that test prep professional development is part of a political-economic milieu that valued financial incentives over her students' best interest. Like Jonathan's acknowledgment that nothing was neutral, Stephanie was able to identify the political motivation behind the mandates.

Neoliberal policies such as mandated, uniform curriculum and high-stakes testing created an ideological environment hostile to SJE. On the school level, such policies were maintained by individual co-workers and administrators who were also operating under fear, reinforcing the CIP members' sense that they were teaching in an environment dominated by compliance.

Within this context, seemingly innocent co-workers unwittingly functioned as traitors or spies to the CIP participants. While these colleagues were most likely well-intentioned and caring educators, their own unwillingness to rock the boat created an environment that made it difficult for the CIP members to implement their social justice curriculum. As a result, the CIP teachers began to finely hone their ability to analyze where their colleagues stood ideologically and to decide whether or not they could risk opening up about their teaching goals. Stephanie reported a story from when she was first setting up her classroom at her school in the Bushwick section of Brooklyn, a school that served mainly Latino children. Another teacher welcomed her by showing her where things were and looking over the class list to give advice and insights into Stephanie's new fifth graders. When reading that a child named Lourdes was in her class, the teacher warned, "Oh, that girl and her mother are going to hate you because you are White."

While this co-teacher was offering what she most likely assumed to be insider and friendly advice, because Stephanie was moving away from Tools of Whiteness she was able to recognize this as bad advice. If Stephanie were to follow this teacher's comment, she would rely on a racialized preconceived idea about Lourdes and not get to know her as an individual. Stephanie exclaimed, "It made me so mad, I mean, if I weren't already thinking from a social justice lens, I might not have liked that student, or I might have treated her differently!" Stephanie's emerging racial lens helped her to see how her colleague's advice functioned as a problematic assumption, serving to maintain racial stereotyping rather than suggesting real strategies to build cross-cultural relationships with her students. Because of the ways in which the CIP teachers were developing a political analysis, they had a harder time relating to their colleagues who were still using the Tools of Whiteness. Examples such as this created unfriendly environments for the participants because, without knowing who to trust or where their colleagues were coming from, the CIPers often found themselves alienated and without support.

Stephanie reported that at first she tried to collaborate with other teachers, and described a time when she showed them a unit that traced the historical routes of racism that led to current racial injustices such as the situation of the Jena Six.[2] Her colleagues reacted by using the Tools of Whiteness to dissuade Stephanie: "They were like, 'Well, this makes White people look bad.' ... We just had arguments about it because they wouldn't teach anything that made White people 'look bad.'" For a young, inexperienced teacher, having veteran school-based colleagues who support your work and provide advice is invaluable. However, Stephanie's colleagues, relying on tools such as those used by the teachers with oppositional stances in Chapter 2, were fearful of teaching about race and created an environment that made her feel alienated because of her commitment to the tenets of social justice that included exposing and addressing historical and current racism.

Being dismissed for trying to do what she felt was right created an unwelcoming environment in which she had few colleagues to turn to for help planning lessons or for help with the kinds of challenges that all first-year teachers experience.

> I don't really talk about it [her curriculum] with them. I don't say, "Let's develop this together" and I feel like they are criticizing me for it. I don't really care, but I do because I guess I want to be respected by the other teachers and I want them to come by my room and be like, "Wow, look what she's doing. This is amazing" whereas I don't always feel like they do that. They are more like, "What is she doing, is she crazy?"

Stephanie found herself craving the support and approval of her peers, but because of her emerging political analysis she became alienated by their use of the Tools of Whiteness and the ways in which they dismissed her commitment to issues of race and inequality.

At other times, Stephanie, like other CIPers, found herself in situations in which she initially felt at ease with her co-workers, only to unwittingly step onto landmines. She reported that one day, while passing time in the teachers' lounge, Stephanie and her colleagues were flipping through the New York *Daily News* and engaging in casual conversation when they came across an article about Barack Obama, who at the time was in the midst of his first election campaign, that claimed he was Muslim.

> I was like, "This is propaganda," and I was saying how the article was trying to make Obama look bad because he was Muslim, and I was like A) He is not Muslim, and B) It's not a bad thing if he was. And the other co-worker

was like, "No, he's got to have some ties with terrorists, and we are all going to get attacked," and I was like, "Never again will I bring that up," because I don't want to have a bad relationship with them and I think, you know, they're good people but they can keep their politics to themselves, and I'm not going to bring that up again.

By innocently expressing her opinion, Stephanie inadvertently stepped onto a landmine that exposed that the ideology of her co-workers was antithetical to her emerging analysis of current issues. This exposed the complex challenge of being committed to social justice while also wanting to have the camaraderie and validation of co-workers that help any new teacher feel accepted at their school. The fear of offending her colleagues kept her in a state of paranoia as she felt she had to watch what she said at all times. Between the ideological imprisonment of mandated curriculum and standardized testing, as well as the spies and landmines at their school sites, these new teachers felt like they always had to watch their backs. With a lack of places to turn to for support within their own schools, they searched to find a place where they could learn and grow with like-minded individuals. Finding such a place in CIP, they committed themselves strongly and used it as a safe space in which to seek respite and reinforcement for their goal of integrating social justice into their curriculum.

Finding Their Place

Because most of their time was spent in their politically charged schools, one of the first things the participants did to protect their goal of teaching for social justice was to find a place for themselves that would feel supportive and safe. They found this place in CIP and used it as a respite from the stress and alienation they felt daily in their schools. As a kindergarten teacher in a Catholic school, Hally shared that she often had to have conversations she found uncomfortable and difficult in order to have her perspective included in the school curriculum. Within the CIP group, she found a protected space to catch her breath and re-energize. She explained, "I think this group is kind of like a winter break. You come here, you get away from it all, and then it motivates you to do better … It lets you separate yourself a little bit." This "break" served to reinforce her commitment and prepared her to re-enter her school with more clarity and strength. Stephanie added:

I would come to the meetings and I would be all over the place, worried about the curriculum and the students and the parents and the administration and I would come here … and it was this group that helped me regain my center and refocus. … Having a place to go where if I felt something was wrong or not being addressed, I can say, "Listen guys, this is messed up," or, "This is what my principal is doing." … Whenever I left here, I was like [takes a deep breath and exhales], I would feel balanced again. I'm excited for our meetings now, that we are going to get to talk.

By finding this place, the CIP members were able to grow as social justice educators because they had people with whom they could discuss tough issues away from their school-based colleagues with whom they often clashed ideologically. They were able to fill key needs that were missing at their schools by supporting each other to develop social justice curricular projects and served as sounding boards for each other's work.

Another way in which the teachers were able to grow as social justice educators was by becoming aware that a broader movement of SJE existed. In the broadest sense, CIP allowed them to feel that their contributions were part of something bigger and that there was strength in numbers. As Nina explained, "Even though I feel like I'm just doing a small little part, and I still feel like I could do a lot more, I feel that what I am doing is something." The feeling Nina described was greatly increased after the group presented at a conference on social justice and teacher education in Chicago. The members were just beginning to see how what they were doing in New York was connected to a national movement of educators who were motivated by social justice and this provided them with a sense of efficacy in their efforts.

Stephanie stated, "Knowing that there are other people out there that want to do the same thing that I now want to do is really exciting and motivating and pushes me almost everyday where I'm like, 'Well, I really don't know if I want to teach this lesson but I will because I *need* to.'" The feeling that she was part of something bigger provided her with a sense of responsibility to a larger movement that fueled Stephanie to push herself further than she would have if she had been on her own. It also helped her to feel that her effort was part of something more powerful. "Before, if I didn't like something, I'd go, 'Well that sucks,' and I didn't realize that other people think it sucks too and we can all get together and do something." Just as one pencil can easily be split in half while a group of pencils is unbreakable, Stephanie realized that by working collectively on issues, she was part of a powerful whole. While she wasn't quite at a point to articulate a sophisticated political analysis about exactly how things "sucked," she did have enough of a sense that something should be done about it. CIPers' new sense of belonging in a broader movement strengthened the members' commitment to teaching about social justice in the classroom. Rather than buying into the nagging sense that they were crazy individuals who were alienated at their schools, they began to understand that they were part of something bigger, a professional movement of caring educators committed to similar goals of SJE.

All the group members believed that without finding their place in CIP and the larger movement, they would not have grown as much as social justice educators. They felt that SJE would have been done in "passing." Jonathan summarized how the group functioned to provide a sense of belonging and accountability. "Maybe none of us would be doing this if we weren't together in it. Don't you feel like it's kind of a club, or kind of like a coalition? I feel that way—it's like a pledge." This pledge that the members made to each other kept them committed to their goal of teaching social justice in unfriendly environments. The next chapter looks more deeply at the role that their reliance on each other to push their social justice agenda played out and how, in some ways, this strategy backfired in moving them to take action outside of the classroom.

Camouflaging Critical Pedagogy

In an attempt to survive the multitude of challenges experienced during the first year of teaching, the CIP members attempted to camouflage their critical pedagogy to keep what they were doing out of the view of others. This allowed them to successfully teach about social justice issues. By substituting alternative materials to integrating themes of equity and justice into the mandated curriculum, the teachers became quite adept at figuring out how to teach within the constraints they faced while still focusing on issues of social justice within their classrooms.

By using the mandated curriculum as a starting point, the participants were able to camouflage the more controversial topics they wished to cover. Inspired by a unit that Hally taught on people without homes, Marissa decided she wanted to introduce the unit to her kindergarten class in a strict Catholic school. She had already been chastised for teaching about Martin Luther King and had constant "visits" to her classroom by administrators and other school personnel. Understanding her context, she decided to disguise the inquiry on poverty within the mandated unit of "families."

According to Marissa, she introduced the unit by talking about her own family and how families are similar and different, focusing particularly on where different families live. She then read the children the book *Fly away Home* (Bunting, 1991), a story about a father and his son who live in an airport because they can't afford a home. "My kids enjoyed talking about this because I really zoomed in on the fact that not all homeless people are alone, but they have families just like them (as one of my kids brought up)." Marissa felt that this helped her students break free of some of the stereotypes they held about people without homes. "They understood that not all homeless people are mean, stink (one of my students shared that her mom thought that), or are starving (shelter homes and food banks)." The project culminated with a showing of the Reading Rainbow video of *Fly away Home*, which also featured children and young teens that lived without homes because of fires or economic problems. By centering this unit on families and by using children's literature, read-alouds, writing webs, and other traditional and mandated forms of literacy instruction, her approach protected her from watchdog colleagues because it appeared that she was teaching a safe unit about families. In reality she was infusing time-honored academic skills with critical topics about poverty and equity with her 5-year-old students.

In another attempt to conceal her social justice curriculum, Marissa used activities that could be deemed as politically neutral as opportunities to challenge students' stereotypes. For example, she shared with CIP that her students held very stereotypical understandings of gender roles, views that were reinforced by school policies such as separating boys and girls for lining up and other activities. To challenge these notions, Marissa built upon an ordinary mathematics lesson on bar graphs by introducing content on gender roles. "What I did was a t-chart and the students named what they thought boys like to do and what girls like to do. We compared the columns, and it was really stereotypes, like girls like dolls." She shared that the next day she listed the activities separately and had the students put checks next to the activities they themselves like to do. The activities did not fall into gender predictive categories as both the boys and the girls in the class enjoyed activities originally assigned to one gender, such as playing with trucks. They used this data to create bar graphs and compared both graphs, contrasting what they thought boys and girls enjoyed with the reality of what they like to do. By using a traditional math activity appropriate for early childhood education, Marissa was able to help her young students develop critical thinking skills and challenge stereotypes while never appearing to have strayed from the mandated math curriculum.

Jonathan and Stephanie, the two fifth-grade teachers in traditional public schools, reported that they were under strict orders and surveillance to execute the mandated literacy curriculum. They both became quite skillful at looking for openings within the curricular structure to integrate social justice themes into their reading and writing blocks. Their most common strategy was to substitute culturally relevant books for the mandated materials. For lessons on "short texts," both chose to use articles from a progressive, independent children's newspaper called *IndyKids* rather than use what Stephanie described as "stupid little books that are just questions and passages, passages and questions."

Both teachers also decided to use the book *Leon's Story* (Tillage, 1997) as part of their mandated character study unit. This book, and their ensuing strategy, had been introduced to them in my social justice education class as undergraduates. *Leon's Story* was written by an African American man reflecting on his experiences growing up in the share cropping South as a child and his experiences in the Civil Rights Movement as a young man. Substituting this book allowed Stephanie and Jonathan to teach about historical oppression while still using the same lesson format that was required by the administrators and coaches who sporadically entered their classrooms to ensure they were at the designated part of the program. The teachers quickly found that, as long as they were addressing the skills required within the units, the administrators were rather indifferent, and sometimes supportive, about the texts they chose. By understanding the administration's priorities, and looking for opportunities to teach social issues while addressing the mandated curriculum, the teachers were able to continue to reach their goal without negative consequences.

Developing Their Students as Activists

Another strategy that a few of these new teachers used while trying to teach social issues was that of teaching their students to be able to analyze and address issues that they faced in their own lives. Unfortunately, not all of the teachers were able to take it this far, as discussed further in Chapter 4, but it is worth sharing one of the successful examples of this strategy. One of the most in-depth social justice projects was completed in Jonathan's classroom. The CACAO Project ("Children Against Chocolate-Aided Oppression") was a semester-long unit that Jonathan and a fellow teacher developed to provide students with multiple experiences with social activism skills: from letter writing, to petitioning, to campaigning, and finally to carrying out a public demonstration. According to Jonathan, the project began simply enough when he and Nick,[3] the other fifth-grade teacher at his school, substituted a test-prep passage with an article about child labor on cocoa farms. After seeing how shocked and angry, yet engaged, their students were with the issue, Jonathan helped his students research more on the topic.

> We looked at the list of companies, and the kids were like "M&M's!" And I said, "Well, what's one thing we could do?" and they were like "We can stop eating M&M's!" and I said "What else can we do?" and it was cool because they were automatic with it: "Get other people to stop eating M&M's!" I was thinking "Right on."

As part of their development, Jonathan wanted to build upon his students' righteous indignation and clear motivation to take action on the issue.

Working with fellow CIP members, the group looked over the scope, sequence, and upcoming units for opportunities to develop further inquiry within the confines of Jonathan's literacy program. During the mandated "realistic fiction" unit, he helped his students imagine what it must be like to be forced to work in intolerable conditions. To develop a sense of empathy, he taught about César Chávez and had students write short stories from the perspective of a fictional child farm worker. Just as Marissa and Hally did in the people without homes unit, Jonathan reframed what could have been a typical charitable approach to one that develops empathy for the purpose of justice.

Next, Jonathan and Nick wanted to provide their students with an opportunity to voice their dissent to the corporations that exploit and benefit from child labor on cocoa farms. Using a curriculum developed by Global Exchange (Schweisguth, n.d.) their students wrote Valentine cards to the CEO of World's Finest Chocolates, a company that is the leading manufacturer of fundraising chocolate but that does not use fair-trade labor practices. These letters easily fit the criteria of the mandated persuasive-essay unit. The cards expressed their anger about child labor on cocoa farms and demanded that the company start using fair-trade practices. Through this part of the unit, the children engaged in a classic activist strategy, power-analysis, to understand which stakeholders were perpetuating and benefiting from this injustice, and to decide what could be done.

The next leg of the mandated curriculum focused on "Social Issues," making it easier to integrate the unit with this segment. The classes learned how to write petitions that they then used to organize their community to persuade the local grocery store to stock fair-trade chocolate. After drafting a compelling petition, collecting over 400 signatures, and hand delivering the petition to the store, the manager happily began stocking the fair-trade candy. The students also worked with the technology teacher to write and create public service announcements, which they filmed and screened for other upper-grade students.

Jonathan and Nick next prepared their students to hold a public demonstration. They watched video footage of other protests, made posters and fliers for the event, called the local police precinct, and then took a field trip to Times Square where the students held a demonstration in front of the M&M/Mars store. The students chanted, held their homemade posters, and passed out their informational fliers to protest the company's use of child labor and to encourage M&M/Mars to use fair-trade practices.

Through the CACAO Project, Jonathan raised his students' consciousness, helped them build empathy with those affected by the injustice, engaged in a power-analysis, and provided concrete skills in letter and petition writing, media production, community organizing, and public demonstration. By providing practice with the hands-on tools and skills of social activism, Jonathan and Nick gave their students opportunities to look critically at the world around them and to take action about injustices that anger them. Because he understood the priorities of his school, he worked within the boundaries of the mandated curriculum, allowing him to enact his goal of teaching about social issues as a form of activism. By integrating this unit within the reading and writing program, Jonathan and Nick won the support of the principal, who was impressed with the blog of the project the teachers created to spread word of their work to other educators.

Going Public

The final strategy was for the teachers to go public with their unwillingness to conform or comply with the pressures found in their schools. Although this was used less frequently than camouflaging, the teachers employed this tactic by rejecting certain school policies, voicing their dissent to colleagues, and teaching their critical pedagogy out in the open. This served to challenge the policies and individuals that continued to make their schools hostile for social justice. By openly questioning or disagreeing with colleagues or policies, the participants invited people to stop complying with mandates and unjust practices by making, or at least exploring, an ideological switch. Examples of going public happened in moments where the participants could have retreated to the protection of the safe haven, but instead felt resilient enough to stand up for their beliefs.

Of all the environments, Marissa's Catholic school was the most restrictive, yet it was she who was the most public with her social justice perspective. Time and time again, Marissa shared stories in which other teachers "popped" into her room to oversee her teaching. She described a colleague: "She comes into my room, pops in all the time. I was teaching about Martin Luther King, and she was just staring at me. She was like, 'Why are you teaching that? You are going to get yourself in so much trouble. Just leave it for some other teacher,'" she said." Rather than "leave it," this watchdog motivated Marissa to speak out at a faculty meeting.

> Just the fact that they tell me "Oh, don't teach that" just makes me want to teach it more now. It's like, "No. We are going to learn it." ... I know it's a Catholic school, but you know, I think there are things that are more important that go beyond prayer. ... I said that at a meeting, I said it goes beyond prayer—it's who you are as a role model. Reality is that it's not by praying that you are going to solve issues. You have to get out there and be aware of your surroundings. ... I told the kids that too.

Marissa stood up to her colleagues who were attempting to get her to comply with the school norms of staying away from social issues. By making her stance public to her faculty, students, and parent communities, she invited them to question themselves and their actions. This served as an advanced strategy because she moved beyond camouflaging and attempted to challenge her non-active colleagues to move away from their own complacency and change what they themselves teach and believe.

In keeping with her comment at the faculty meeting, Marissa kept her SJE public. She still used the strategy of beginning with the mandated curriculum as her starting point, but she did so out in the open, in plain view of other teachers and families. "I am drawing together Malcolm X with the [required] fairness unit. I wrote to the parents and told them that we are using great books, they can read them, the pictures match the words, and also it brings an important message. I put it right in my parent communication that I do everyday." Because Marissa was excited about and committed to this unit, she felt bolstered to share the details of the project openly.

While many of the parents had positive reactions ("Good job, My kid was telling me about Malcolm X when I was showering him!"), many of her co-workers did not. Marissa didn't allow negative reactions from these teachers deter her. She described her heritage month unit: "I didn't even close my door for this. I was like, 'I'm going to leave it open and if they hear it, they hear it.' Special education teachers would come in and pull my kids, and they would just sit and stare." Rather than stop her lesson, Marissa went on to describe how she would have her students engage the stunned visitors in a conversation about the topic. Despite the reactions of her co-teachers, Marissa said that her principal did not interfere in her classroom and Marissa never changed her focus. By keeping her pedagogy public, Marissa refused to give in to a climate of fear and silencing. She stood up against the conservative ideology of her school by demanding that people be aware of the kind of critical pedagogy that is possible with young children.

Conclusion

By building a safe haven to protect their vision and developing strategies such as camouflaging, developing their students as activists, and going public, the teachers in this chapter were successful in accomplishing a key characteristic of SJE—teaching about social issues. As a result, their students had opportunities to investigate current and historical oppression, they learned how to research issues of injustice, they made connections to their own lives, and they engaged in some types of social action.

By using these strategies, these emerging social justice teachers were able to create a context that supported them to enact the goal of teaching about social issues. There were several factors that allowed this, factors that can support other new teachers to further their political analysis and integrate social issues into their curriculum. One factor was that there was a long-standing relationship between the members of the group and myself as the facilitator, which helped the teachers to have a strong degree of trust, allowing us to push each other further.

The teachers, all members of the same cohort of undergraduates, were all at the same stage of their careers and had transitioned together from students to new professionals, helping them to feel a sense of camaraderie and equality. This was important as they began to talk about tough issues that had been "taboo" topics of conversation for many of them prior to CIP. Without having this sense of safety, they may not have been able to have had a space to begin to explore issues or historical events that helped to shape their emerging political analysis, which in turn informed the curriculum they developed.

Along with trust in each other, the teachers trusted the direction in which I led the group because of my experience as a classroom teacher in urban settings, my work as an organizer with NYCoRE, a teacher activist group, as well as being someone who had supported them for the last three years as their undergraduate professor. Through constant check-ins, shared agenda and schedule setting, goal and norm setting, I was able to set into place structures that allowed the participants to feel more ownership over CIP than in a more generic professional development project. This attempt toward shared leadership allowed me to hold multiple roles with the participants, from mentor, to friend, to someone who held them accountable to the social justice goals they had set. This allowed the teachers to see themselves as professionals, which subsequently supported them to feel more confident in their political stance in their schools. Creating trust like this in groups such as CIP is essential so that teachers have support as they take the often intimidating steps of moving against the ideological norms of their colleagues.

For those interested in teaching for social justice, these successes, however, are bittersweet. On the one hand, what these CIP participants accomplished was no small feat considering that they were young, inexperienced teachers working in conditions that did not support the kind of teaching they wanted to do. By having access to a network of supportive peers, these teachers were able to integrate social issues into their classrooms, unlike many of their contemporaries.

These are teachers who entered the profession with the hopes of "making a differ-ence" and contributing to positive change in society. However, the constraints they faced within public schools made it difficult for them to realize their idealism, leading to frustration, a lack of efficacy, and attrition. Research on teacher attrition shows that a key group of educators who leave the profession are teachers like the ones in this study, who could be described as "service oriented" and "idealistic" (Miech & Elder, 1996). CIP and the strategies that this group developed may have helped to keep such social justice-oriented teachers in the classroom longer than if they did not have this kind of support. All of the teachers in this chapter returned to the classroom the following year, and the enrollment in the project more than doubled the following year. Given the statistics on new teacher attrition, over half of them should have left by now.[4] Of all the teachers that participated in CIP over the course of its five years, only one has left the classroom, and that was to enter graduate school for school leadership and advocacy. By building their safe haven and developing strategies, it appears as if the teachers in this study found an outlet to funnel their frustration and alienation, and establish efficacy in ways that contributed to their ability to navigate the unsupportive environment that other teachers are unable to thrive in.

On the other hand and as will be discussed further in the next chapter, these strategies as a whole did little to transform the larger forces that are waging a war for control over public education. As Montano, et al. (2002) point out, working solely within the classroom is but one component of SJE. While it may be all that we can hope for with new teachers, working on curriculum will have little impact on the existing power structure. When we consider neoliberal forces such as privatization and corporate control as some of the enemies of educational justice (Anyon, 2005; Kumashiro, 2008), then simply substituting readings about school segregation may be a successful strategy for integrating social issues in the classroom, but it is not a tactic that will actually address institutional racism. An additional danger with the strategies used by the teachers in this study is that they can provide a false sense of satisfaction that what they are doing is "enough"; in reality the context they are teaching remains just as menacing to the well-being of students.

This dilemma of not working to change root causes of oppression has serious implications for those concerned with using SJE as a vehicle for equity and change. The findings from this chapter reveal that while emerging social justice educators can be successful at creating classrooms in which students learn about social issues and have occasional opportunities for action, without larger forays into social move-ments or activism, these teachers are fighting a losing battle, as they are not transform-ing the broader neoliberal agenda (Anyon, 2005; Oakes & Lipton, 2007). If teachers continue to work as individuals in their classrooms, they can make the confines of their narrowing academic freedom more palatable, but they are doing little to stop the continuing invasion of corporate takeovers of schools. You can decorate a jail cell, but you still aren't free. By creatively adapting their classroom practice, teachers impact only the effects of the neoliberal policies, and not the root causes that will continue to bear down on schools, making ongoing strategies that much more difficult to negotiate.

The teachers who joined CIP were at a beginning stage of developing a political analysis about social injustice. Like the teachers in Chapter 2, many did not have life opportunities in which they learned to critically recognize injustice nor engage in activism prior to joining CIP. Only one among them, Nina, regularly engaged in social activism in their own lives. However, the teachers in this chapter all had a sense that injustice was wrong and they felt that the best strategy to address it was to teach about it. In that sense, they were successful at reaching their goal. They wanted to be the kind of teachers who taught about social justice. They were not quite ready, however, to be the kind of people who wanted to work to change the conditions that caused social injustice in their daily lives. Part of this was because they had not yet developed a fully realized vision of a world without injustice that would allow them to understand and target the forces that create the inequality that they had begun to recognize. Without such a vision, it was difficult for them to know where to start or what to do to push further than their classroom, leaving the inequality that they were concerned about in place. The next chapter explores this dilemma in more detail.

4

STUCK AT THE CLASSROOM DOOR
Falling Back on Tools of Inaction

As seen in the last chapter, these new young teachers in CIP did an excellent job of integrating their developing understanding of inequality into their classroom curriculum. The process of integrating issues of social justice with the mandated curriculum was a skill in which they became increasingly adept. They were successful in this one key component of social justice education (SJE): creating classrooms in which their students critically analyzed social issues on a regular basis. Despite the fact that they were young teachers with little experience with social justice issues, the members were successful at finding resources, and figuring out how to integrate social issues into their elementary school curricula.

The next logical steps in their journey would have been to become teacher activists by moving outside of the classroom door to engage their students in social action and to develop as activists themselves. Without such efforts, teachers such as the CIPers will never impact the conditions they teach about and that they profess to be against. By only teaching about social issues, the CIPers raise awareness about the symptoms of injustice, but never impact the roots, creating an endless cycle. Unfortunately, the CIP teachers admittedly provided few to no opportunities for their students to address root causes by engaging in action in sustained ways, and they themselves rarely used their time outside of the classroom to work for social change.

Two components of SJE that appear less frequently in the literature are 1) how teachers can engage young people in actively transforming their communities and worlds (Christensen, 2009; Freire, 1970; Duncan-Andrade & Morrell, 2008), and 2) how teachers can become activists themselves (Montano, *et al.*, 2002; Marshall & Anderson, 2009). While there is literature that raises the importance of teachers stepping outside of the school to engage in social justice activism in the community and broader society (Giroux, 1988; Kincheloe, 2005), there are few teachers taking on this role and there are fewer professional development opportunities that actually prepare or support teachers to engage in this component of being a social justice educator.

The teachers themselves actually acknowledged that this was a goal that they weren't reaching as of yet. While they weren't comfortable with this fact, they were aware that they weren't moving to the next step of becoming teacher activists. This chapter examines why this did not happen as expected by examining findings from the third year of CIP, which at this point consisted of ten members all of whom were first-, second-, and third-year teachers. Nine of the ten participants graduated from 2007–9 cohorts of the undergraduate program[1] and they taught in six different schools in a variety of communities in New York City, with the exception of Luis, who taught in urban New Jersey, and Nancy, who taught in Long Island, NY.

The teachers in this iteration of CIP had the knowledge to know that they should be moving forward in the arena of activism, but, at the same time, they were aware that this wasn't happening. This created a tension for them. The CIP teachers had two choices, to embrace the difficulty of this challenge and dedicate themselves to growing as activists, or acknowledge that they weren't meeting all of their goals of SJE and retreat back to the comfort of the classroom. Unfortunately, more often than not, the CIPers retreated using a specific set of tools to justify their actions.

Tools of Inaction

To not feel like failures when asked about the areas in which they felt they were less successful, the teachers used "Tools of Inaction" to try to relieve the tension caused by not taking the next steps out of the classroom. When discussing the reasons for why they weren't engaging in social action, the teachers recognized that they had no excuse. Most members expressed these comments: "It's just my fault, I mean I can't really blame anyone or say anything," "I need to just do it, I need to stop making excuses," "I don't really have a legitimate excuse." While they recognized that there was no excuse, they offered a series of reasons, or Tools of Inaction, for why they were falling short.

These tools, as seen in Table 4.1, fell into four categories that served to justify the standstill: 1) Tools of Substitution were used to explain that, while the teachers

TABLE 4.1 Tools of Inaction

Substitution	Postponement	Displacement	Dismissal
I'm rocking it in the classroom	What's my issue?	You have to make us	I can't make a difference
Teaching is action	I'll do something when it affects me	I don't want to go alone	I have a life
	I'm a new teacher	No one follows through	
		It's because of the kids	

weren't working on action *per se*, they were spending time and effort on something else of import, typically their teaching. 2) Tools of Postponement were used to explain the reasons why the teachers could not take action in the present, and served as a promise to take action at some point in the future. 3) Tools of Displacement were used to place the blame of inaction on someone else. 4) Tools of Dismissal were used to explain away the need for them to take action at all.

Taken together, Tools of Inaction allowed the teachers to relieve the emotional discomfort they experienced by not taking action. Unlike the teachers who used the Tools of Whiteness, these teachers *did* recognize inequality and wanted to do something about it, as evidenced in the last chapter. They couldn't unsee the things they had accepted, or in some cases experienced, in terms of oppression and injustice; nor did they want to. However, both sets of tools functioned to keep their users stuck in their current stage of development, serving to release their responsibility for working for change and ultimately maintaining inequality.

Because the Tools of Inaction helped the teachers to feel okay with their inactivity, it released them from feeling the tension between the world they wanted to see and the world as it is. The chapter that follows this one shows how working to reconcile a vision with reality, rather than retreat from it, is what drives the work of experienced teacher activists. In contrast, by using the Tools of Inaction, the CIP teachers blocked themselves from participating more fully in social change. In order to become fully realized teacher activists, the CIPers would need to recognize their use of these Tools of Inaction and actively embrace these tensions as a driving force that could move them outside of the classroom door. This chapter examines these Tools of Inaction and the impact they have on teachers who profess to want to create change, but seem to hit roadblocks in their development toward teacher activism.

Tools of Substitution

Tools of Substitution are common tools that we use when avoiding something that we aren't excited about doing. How many times do I start tweaking my syllabi for upcoming courses rather than grade my current students' papers? By working on my syllabi, something I enjoy and can do with ease, I justify not grading, something I find more arduous. I can feel all right about this form of substitution because I am still being productive. It's not like I'm watching television! By using this Tool of Substitution, I can feel okay about not doing what I actually need to focus on because I am working on something else related and important. For CIPers, the Tools of Substitution allowed them to alleviate the guilt and discomfort they felt about not taking action by helping them feel active in related and important ways. The CIPers knew that they were not engaging in action and felt some guilt about it, but they were still developing social justice curriculum and engaging in other activities connected to their developing consciousness. They owned their lack of action, and recognized that they had no valid excuses for it. However, they used the Tools of Substitution to feel better about their lack of action, highlighting these other activities instead.

"I'm Rocking It in the Classroom"

Often CIPers substituted social action with the work of teaching. When asked what areas of SJE they were not making progress on, members readily admitted that they were not taking social action personally—as a group or with students. In admitting this, however, they were quick to mention their classroom teaching about inequality.

Shifting the focus from what they had not accomplished to what they had done allowed the teachers to feel better about their inaction. As Reina said, "I am actually feeling like I got this curriculum thing down. The integrating stuff I'm good at, I'm doing it all the time and I'm rocking it, but the action part is not happening yet." This substitution allowed Reina to reflect on past successes rather than on future actions.

Often when CIPers recognized that they were not engaging students in activism, they shifted the focus to what they had done. Stephanie demonstrated:

> We're all committed to making our kids more passionate and empathetic and aware and conscious and critical … and I think I am doing that in my classroom and I think other people are too, and I think we're all just not taking that extra step. We haven't reached as CIP that … level of social justice [where we take social action].

Like other members, Stephanie felt good about the curricular components of her SJE, even while admitting that she wasn't taking the step of activism. In keeping with this Tool of Substitution, she shifted the focus from a discussion on activism to what she did in her classroom. While CIP used a framework of SJE that included social action, Stephanie referred to that step as "extra" rather than a core component.

The participants were well aware of the success they had with integrating social justice into the curriculum. They presented at national conferences, guest taught in pre-service classes, and wrote a book chapter about their pedagogy.[2] Surprisingly these activities actually served to impede the groups' progress toward activism, lulling the group into feeling prematurely accomplished. Because their classroom work was well received, they felt confident and comfortable engaging in this kind of work, and ended up privileging it rather than risk moving into the unchartered territory of social action. The substitution tool of "I'm rocking it in the classroom" made the participants feel more able to claim the identity of social justice educator without engaging in frequent, and typically painful, critical reflection about the areas in which they were falling short.

"Teaching is Action"

By using the "I'm rocking it in the classroom" tool, the teachers allowed their classroom work to trump a focus on action. The "Teaching is action" tool entirely replaced the demand for action by claiming teaching and action were one and the same. Some CIPers expressed that they didn't know they were supposed to engage in action because teaching about social issues felt sufficient. In keeping with the literature about multicultural and culturally relevant education (Ladson-Billings, 1994; Cochran-Smith, 2004), much of what is asked of teachers happens within the classroom. This helped lead to the sense that teaching is action. As Jonathan explained, "I think a lot of us were satisfied with the idea that sharing our work, presenting at conference, working with children was social action." By using teaching is action, the teachers released themselves from the responsibility of bringing SJE outside of the classroom.

In fairness to participants, most of how we used our time during CIP was on curriculum development. That they were even teaching about social issues put them light-years ahead of their school-based colleagues on a continuum of SJE. This added to the CIPers' sense that they were doing enough. They sincerely wanted to do something to challenge inequality but, because of the newness of their own developing political analysis about how oppression operates, they believed that their action in the classroom, such as teaching about current events, childhood obesity, and homelessness, was addressing inequality.

However, by equating teaching with activism, the target of the teachers' actions was their students, not root causes or manifestations of inequality. CIPers were successful at raising their students' awareness about injustices, but the teachers didn't engage in activities that might actually challenge root causes. As a result, they supported their students to be more capable of negotiating unjust conditions, rather than developing strategies or joining efforts to change those conditions. For example, when teaching students about nutrition, the teachers taught the students about how to make the best choices out of the abysmal lunch offerings in the cafeteria, instead of taking the risks to challenge the school and district to provide food that was actually healthy for their students.

Many social justice educators believe that teaching the next generation is a form of social action, and I don't disagree. However, this tool was used to let CIPers off the hook of stepping outside of the classroom themselves, substituting the responsibility for social action onto their young students. The tool of "Teaching is action" resulted in teaching students to negotiate injustice rather than change it, and removed the responsibility of action by helping the teachers feel satisfied with their curricular accomplishments.

Tools of Postponement

The Tools of Postponement were used to explain away the teachers' inaction as a byproduct of their current situation. The presumption here was that, once their temporary circumstances changed, they would be better able to take action. By using tools that claimed they did not know "what issues they cared about," or that they "needed to master first-year teaching," CIPers felt better about their inaction because it was just a temporary state, one that would be resolved shortly.

"What's My Issue?"

When explaining why they weren't more active, most of the participants' responses revealed either a lack of direct connection to issues of social (in)justice or a lack of a sense that there is something that can or should be done about it. This was evident in the multiple responses that explained that they did not know what issues they felt strongly about. As Melanie explained:

> I need to figure out what I'm really passionate about. … Like I'm interested in gay marriage, but then I'm really interested in other things, like everything! I feel like I need to focus more … I can't do this, this and this, but I want to do something. I need to find out what that "something" is for me.

While it's clear that Melanie has the desire to do something about a variety of issues, the fact that she does not know where to focus reveals a lack of connection to issues of social injustice. She is aware of issues, and expresses that she wants to do something, but, rather than being driven to act out of an intense sense of necessity or survival, she takes an approach that is more intellectual in nature because of her lack of experiences with social injustice.

Similarly, in discussing why she hasn't yet taken social action, Stephanie shows how not knowing what issue she wants to work on serves as a Tool of Postponement. In discussing her next steps, she says she needs to start "educating myself on the current issues and then picking one to be part of changing." While Stephanie clearly sees a need and desire to figure out her "issue," she uses a Tool of Postponement by saying "Those are definitely the very clear, logical next steps, something that I will hopefully be doing this summer." Because she isn't directly impacted by social injustice, it is unclear what issue she wants to take action on, and she reflects on it as almost an academic exercise. By using the "What's my issue?" tool, the teachers are able to construct their inaction as a temporary state; they will take action as soon as they find time to figure out their passion.

This tool allowed CIPers to distance themselves from social injustice by treating it as a project on their to-do list that they can postpone for a more convenient time ("hopefully this summer"). The tool of "What's my issue?" is in stark contrast to the fully realized teacher activists in the next chapter whose political analysis drives how they make decisions about what to take action on. Such teachers are able to analyze the forces oppressing their students and their classrooms, and take action on these issues. The CIP teachers had a harder time seeing the connections between forces shaping inequality and where to direct their potential activism.

"I'll Do Something When It Affects Me"

Because of the lack of personal connection that many, although not all, of the participants had to social injustice, they often saw it as other people's problems. In contrast, the tool of "I'll do something when it affects me" demonstrated that, when issues did directly affect them, the teachers were less likely to postpone action. Jonathan explained:

> Most of the people in the group haven't been worrying about anything like this [social justice] for very long, so when it does come to your door, it is much more pressing than when you're just reading about it. I think there's something about teaching in a city like this where it's like, "out of sight, out of mind."

Jonathan recognized that, because of some of their social positionality as people less affected by social injustice, it was easier to distance themselves from action. However, when injustice "comes to your door," postponement seemed to be less of an option. Based on what the CIPers initially claimed, it would seem that, when they were affected, they would step up.

At the time of the interviews, the New York City Department of Education (NYCDOE) was threatening all new teachers with pink slips because of budgetary issues. When asked how potential pink slips would affect how they might participate in protests organized about this, Maya responded, "This is my job, this is my life, what am I going to do? To have it affect me makes it much more real, and makes me want to do something about it, rather than if it's just happening to someone else." The tool, "I'll do something when it affects me," demonstrates that a direct connection with social injustice seemed to make the teachers less likely to postpone action then when inequality is "just happening to someone else." From what Maya said, it would seem that she and other members would be banging down the doors of City Hall at the protest organized at this issue that affected "her job" and "her life." Ironically, however, while most CIPers said they would attend the rally, only Nick and Reina actually came.

Three members did seem to move away from postponing action when they were affected. The teachers who did have concrete examples of taking social action participated in causes connected either to their own school, life, or identity. Nick became active in fighting to keep his school from being further overcrowded when the NYCDOE announced that another school was to move in to his building. Reina, a religious Jewish woman, participated in several pro-Israeli actions[3] and Chantale, a Haitian American woman, went on a church-organized mission to Haiti after the devastation of the earthquake of 2010. While these activities do show that some of the members *did* take social action in their own lives, it also confirms that being personally connected to issues of perceived injustice increased the likelihood of action.

Taken together, the tools of "What's my issue?" and "I'll take action when it affects me" reveal a fundamental dilemma in efforts to transform mainstream teachers into activists. Can the typically White and middle-class teachers (US Department of Education, 2008) that work in urban schools feel the connection with communities different from their own that appears to be a prerequisite to stop postponing activism? While it seems clear that the teachers in Chapter 2 who actively use Tools of Whiteness are not in a place to do this, is that the case even with these emerging social justice educators? Without a core belief system that holds "an injustice anywhere is a threat to injustice everywhere" (King, 1963), even the emerging social justice teachers fall back on tools that make their participation in issues that affect "someone else" less likely. Without the sense of urgency and drive of feeling personally invested in social change, the teachers relied on these Tools of Postponement to feel better about their inaction.

"I'm a New Teacher"

Adjusting to the challenges of first-year teaching in addition to becoming a social justice educator often proved to be overwhelming for newer group members. They relied on the "I'm a new teacher" Tool of Postponement to feel better about this dilemma. The first-year participants said they had to postpone integrating social justice until they got situated. As Melanie said, "Being a first-year teacher and a first-year social justice educator, I don't know if I was ready for all of that at once." The assumption was that once they become grounded in the classroom, they would be ready for action.

For some of the second- and third-year teachers, their ability to integrate social justice into curriculum certainly did improve over time, but simply getting the first year under their belt did not provide the push toward action. Luis expressed that "I think being a new teacher, even though it's my third year, it's been really tough. ... I feel like I'm still working on that [SJE curriculum], trying to get it down, get that settled before I jump into other things, but I'm not really sure if that's taking me anywhere." Despite being a third-year teacher, Luis still used this Tool of Postponement. This tool helped the teachers feel better about their inaction; it served as a promise of what they would do in the future, releasing them from the responsibility of the present. As Luis's admission that he wasn't sure if postponement was working demonstrates, this tool is limited by an expiration date, which offers hope that the initial comfort it provides will wear off, pushing teachers toward action.

Tools of Displacement

The next set of tools served to shift the blame of the teachers' inaction from themselves onto others: to CIP itself, to colleagues, to students, or to each other. These tools highlight the fact that at this point CIPers had not internalized a drive for justice or action and relied on external pressure to push them forward. In lieu of any such pressure, the teachers displaced the responsibility of their inaction onto others.

"You Have to Make Us"

When asked why they didn't participate in action, several participants displaced responsibility for taking action from themselves to an external force that should push them to be more active. Nancy said, "I feel like sometimes we are like little kids; you have to put it out in front of us … maybe saying, 'here's an event' or even making it a requirement, attending one event every two months." Similarly, Chantale added, "It's sort of like a training; people need to be kind of taken into the ring and told 'this is us, this is what we're doing.' … I mean you can't force people to do stuff, but just know the expectation." If CIP had better "training" or required members to attend events, then participants felt they would have taken more action. Moving the responsibility from themselves to their training points to these teachers' sense that the motivation to participate in activism is something extrinsic to themselves, rather than an internal value or drive.

The tool of "You have to make us" is particularly dangerous because it inhibits the development of an internal drive toward justice and activism. In the current context of education, there is no shortage of demands put on teachers in terms of testing, accountability, paperwork, etc. However, there are few administrators who are going to "make" teachers be accountable to equity and justice. Without the development of an internal drive, it is less likely that the CIPers' expressed desire to work toward justice will be sustainable. Despite their calls for it, strategies for developing activists such as requirements, accountability, and training are antithetical to a justice-oriented stance in which people see the core of their own well-being tied up with the suffering of others. Compared with the teachers introduced in the next chapter, the CIPers lacked an independent vision of justice and change. This vision was the very reason the teacher activists in Chapter 5 relied on to wake up in the morning to work for a more just world through consistent, sustained, and collective action. Without this vision, the CIPers stalled in their movement outside of the classroom.

"I Don't Want to Go Alone"

When offering reasons why the participants did not seem to be able to take that next step, a common response was that they experienced fear and anxiety about taking the risks they associated with social action. Because of their lack of familiarity with attending events associated with activism, they were often afraid to attend meetings or events alone. Part of why some teachers such as Nick had not participated stemmed from mistrust of the intention of activists. He said, "You don't know who's going to be there. An email might say it's a protest about one thing, but when you show up it might be something totally different." By making assumptions about potential hidden agendas of such groups, the teachers were able to distance themselves, relieving some of the pressure of feeling like they had to attend.

Their mistrust and lack of familiarity made them feel extremely uncomfortable showing up to these settings, particularly alone. As Nancy explained, "When it comes to something like this [attending rallies], I haven't really done it, so just to go with someone who's in a similar situation would be a more comfortable thing." Similarly, many of the teachers suggested that if CIPers attended events together, they would be more likely to go. Luis said, "If we had buddies or a little group, I think it would be easier and that might change the way we see CIP. ... It's hard to go to things by yourself, it's just hard."

Consistent with the tool of "You have to make us," the teachers' fear of attending alone stopped them from participating in the multiple events that either I myself had helped to organize or that they learned about through various sources. If they did attend something, it was usually a one-time occurrence such as a film screening or a speaker; these teachers typically did not join organizations or ongoing campaigns. By feeling like they would go only if they had a "buddy," they displaced the need to go alone. They used this tool with the following tool, "No one follows through," to ensure that they wouldn't have to go because they couldn't find someone to go with them, further displacing responsibility onto their peers.

"No One Follows Through"

Connected to their fear of attending events alone, the tool of "No one follows through" was used to place some of the responsibility of not attending onto their peers' lack of commitment to the group. When members did try to seek out peers to take action together, they often received no reply, causing them to be disappointed and less likely to reach out again in the future. As Nick lamented, "I've sent out emails about things, and you and Stephanie were the only ones to show up [to protests at] my school. I know people are busy, but I don't know. ... " This sense of disappointment was felt most strongly by Reina, who had to travel to Chicago alone after she was the only one who purchased airfare for a conference that the group had all committed to attending together. She had worked through some of her frustration about this and grew to become excited at our two-day weekend retreat in January when the entire group became "fired up" about taking social action after watching *The People Speak*, an inspiring Howard Zinn documentary about how ordinary citizens provoked change. However, this excitement was quickly extinguished:

> I think everybody left the retreat by saying, "Okay, let's go, we're ready!" but I don't think everybody really wanted to actually take that next step and I felt very, very frustrated that I was sending out emails [about events and protests] because that was what we had all said we wanted to do, and then there was

no response and I was like, "Okay, maybe this group isn't the group of people that I want to go do this with." ... After the retreat, I was like, "There's no excuse—this is ridiculous."

For some members, the lack of follow-through from their peers served as an excuse for them to avoid taking action as individuals. This allowed them to displace responsibility for action from themselves to CIP, which they interestingly began to see as a place that hindered their activism, rather than a place that pushed them to move forward in a safe and supportive way.

For some members, such as Nick and Reina, however, the tool of "No one follows through" seemed to actually provoke action in that the frustration and sense of irritation was enough to drive them out of the inertia of the group toward taking action as individuals. In fact, Reina decided to leave CIP when the school year ended, claiming that she wanted to find a group that was more responsive to taking action, rather than to continue to displace responsibility onto her peers.

"It's Because of the Kids"

The final area where some of the teachers displaced responsibility for taking social justice action within their classrooms involved their students. For Luis, who taught sixth to eighth grade special education, it seemed that he had difficulty developing the classroom management skills needed to pull off social justice projects. "These kids are really hard to engage. ... It just took all my energy and I was like, 'Oh my god, if I can't even get them to shut up for five minutes, how can I get them to get motivated about stuff outside their world?'"

For Nick, it was less about management, and more about figuring out what he felt was age-appropriate in terms of action for his second graders. "In terms of action with my class, I'm not sure what to do with them. They are only seven. So we can letter write and we've done that, but I don't think they'd ever be ready for a protest." Stephanie added to this theme when she reported that only "good" students should participate in actions and protests:

> I like bringing the kids that I know get it and why we are doing it. There is a purpose, and not all the kids really understand why [they would attend a protest] and they just think it's fun to yell and scream. And that could be my fault or it could be them not taking in whatever I'm teaching, but I definitely feel that I want to leave that privilege [of attending rallies] or the special things that we do for the kids that really, truly understand why we're there.

The tool of "It's because of the kids" shows a lack of faith in their students' ability to be motivated, capable, or intellectually ready to participate in social action. Because of this lack of faith, teachers excuse both the students and themselves from taking action. The tool creates a serious detriment to these teachers' willingness to provide opportunities for social action for their students and points to deeper concerns with their expectations for their students in general.

Seeing social action as a "privilege," as Stephanie called it, for only the students who appear to understand the issue is in direct conflict with Duncan-Andrade's (2007) construct of five pillars of effective urban teachers. His first pillar of critically conscious purpose contends that effective teachers approach their classrooms with the belief that their low-income students of Color, who are the most marginalized, are the most likely to become powerful agents of change. The teachers in Duncan-Andrade's (2007) study "recognized that the students most likely to change the world were also the ones most likely to struggle in a typical classroom environment" (p. 625). In contrast, CIPers' distrust of their students' ability to care about, understand, or participate against social injustice disenfranchised the teachers' most powerful allies in their expressed desire to create change. Not only do they not take their students to participate, but it also lets the teachers off the hook from venturing outside the classroom. The tool of "It's because of the kids" displaces the blame of not providing students with opportunities for social change onto the students themselves, relieving the teachers from having to see why their own hesitations were actually responsible for their standstill in taking social action.

Tools of Dismissal

The final set of tools that release people from taking action, Tools of Dismissal, expressed the participants' concern that social action was ineffective, and therefore made them feel more comfortable in their choice not to participate in it. The teachers failed to recognize other forms of social action outside of protesting, which many of them dismissed as ineffective, and therefore not worth their time. Because they had not yet developed a more nuanced analysis about how social change operates, the teachers relied on mainstream constructions of "the natural social order" of inequality and the sense that it is too enormous to transform. Similar to the Tool of Whiteness of "What do you expect me to do about it?" from Chapter 2, this tool made them feel that, because they couldn't create a socially just world, it was almost a waste of time to take any action.

"I Can't Make a Difference"

Despite watching, reading about, and even meeting successful teacher activists, it seemed that these CIPers did not have faith in the power of social movements or individuals to transform unjust conditions. Because they felt powerless, they used the tool "I can't make a difference" to dismiss participating in something that they thought was hopeless. When asked if she would participate in protests against the lay-offs that threatened her position, Stephanie responded, "I think another thing that gets in my way is my sense of efficacy. I don't really think that my participating will change anything. That's hard to say, but it's true. I feel really small." Not unlike the other teachers, Stephanie had doubts that social action, and specifically her participation in it, could create change. The logical response therefore was inaction. In contrast to Frederick Douglass's (1857) declaration that "power concedes nothing without a demand," the participants believed that "If power concedes nothing *even with* a demand, why bother demanding?"

While some members' sense that they couldn't make a difference was driven by their lack of familiarity with social justice, Luis's fear was centered in his familiarity of injustice. As an immigrant who moved to the United States as a child, Luis had first-hand experience with inequality, which created his fear to participate.

> [It's] a fear of not being able to make change. That's why I haven't really engaged in it. It's just too painful because I'm an immigrant and I know what it is. My father was an illegal immigrant and just seeing all this injustice in this country, it's scary and it makes me feel hopeless and I think that's why I haven't really stepped up.

Luis' fear, rooted in his experiences, served as protection from the pain of being unable to create change as well as a roadblock from trying. If he doesn't make the commitment to attempt to create change, then it won't hurt as much if he does not experience a victory and change doesn't happen. The mainstream ideology of "nothing you can do about it" was operating in this tool, allowing the teachers to dismiss action because they felt that activism felt as pointless as spitting in the wind.

"I Have a Life"

The final dismissal tool, "I have a life," was used to address the challenge that all teachers face: balancing their work with their personal life. The teachers were overwhelmed with the newness of teaching and their other competing priorities. Events and responsibilities in their personal lives were often cited as reasons why they couldn't attend particular events ("I wanted to go to the union event, but I was signing my lease") but were also used as a broader umbrella of why they generally dismissed activism. Luis explained: "People are very individual. We all say 'Oh we have things to do, we have this and this.' But really, nobody puts their heart into it because they're so, take it from me, I'm so involved in my own things." Because of their involvement with their "own things," activism was seen as a choice, or a chore, and typically not the most attractive one.

It was true that the participants were busy and over-committed people. Some taught after-school, tutored, volunteered, were in committed relationships, and one member was a parent. When it came to committing their limited free time to participating in activism, it often lost out to other options. By expressing their over-commitment, they validated their decision not to be active because they felt justified in their choices. Nancy said, "I want to do it [activism], but that's not the number one thing that I want to do, and if I actually have these two hours where I could go to this thing that I've never done anything with before, or like sleep for a change, sometimes sleep would win out." Jonathan demonstrated that "I'm protective of my personal time. I'm not always good at cutting it up into things that are immediately less fun." In these statements, activism was a chore or responsibility—not the number one thing they would like to do.

This sense of activism as an "immediately less fun" option is in contrast to the personal satisfaction that many activists feel about their work. On the contrary, the teacher activists in the next chapter explicitly claimed that their engagement in activism was not a choice; in fact they described it as a calling, the direct opposite of how the CIPers constructed it through this tool. CIPers saw activism as "extra" and constructed participation as a choice, rather than a drive that fueled their work and behavior. By using "I have a life," the CIP teachers created a binary in which their life existed in one area, and social justice existed, or did not exist, elsewhere.

Conclusion

The emerging educators in the last two chapters were at a particular moment of development on a continuum of social justice teacher activists. Unlike the teachers in Chapter 2, the CIP teachers recognized that inequality was wrong, and they wanted to do something about it as educators. Because they saw their involvement in social justice as classroom based, their solution to addressing inequality was to teach about it, and, as seen in Chapter 3, they successfully integrated social issues into their curriculum.

Having had only limited exposure to social inequality, mainly in their undergraduate education, and inconsistently through their lived experiences, these CIPers were just in the beginning stages of developing their conscious awareness of how oppression and social change operate. Most of the CIP teachers, even those who had faced oppression in their own lives, were new to the concept that something could be done about injustice. Luis, an immigrant who experienced great injustice in his own educational background as an ESL student, expressed, "I didn't really know what social justice was when I joined CIP, the full extent of it, what it really is. I was exposed to it with you [as an undergraduate student], so when I joined the team, I didn't really know what the steps were." Unlike the teachers in Chapter 2, the CIPers had developed a sense in their coursework that inequality existed and it was wrong, and they joined CIP because they realized they wanted to do something about it.

From this perspective, it is easy to understand why they would think that their teaching was action in and of itself. They wanted to do something about inequality, and they were: they were teaching about it in their classrooms. However, when it came time for them to move beyond the classroom door to affect actual change on issues of social injustice, they became stuck and used Tools of Inaction to lessen the burden they felt. These tools helped the participants to feel better: the Tools of

Substitution made them feel good about what they had accomplished; the Tools of Postponement allowed them to believe they would act in the future; the Tools of Displacement transferred responsibility to others; and finally, the Tools of Dismissal swept away the effectiveness of activities in which they did not wish to involve themselves.

One of the major factors causing the CIP teachers' inaction was the ways in which they envisioned social change. Because of the way they themselves learned about American progress, the CIP teachers believed that social change happened as one big "win." When they learned history, the focus was only on the win: the emancipation proclamation ending slavery, the signing of the 19th amendment granting women the right to vote, "the" March on Washington (which of course referred to the March in 1968 in which Martin Luther King gave his "I Have a Dream" speech, not the countless marches that happen there every weekend). They never learned about the ongoing meetings, failures, disappointments, and struggles that lead up to those big wins. Rather than see social change as a lifelong struggle with small wins and losses along the way, the CIPers were unsure of how to participate because an opportunity to take part in such a historic "winning" event did not present itself. As will be explored in the next chapter, fully realized teacher activists understand that social change is not about a big "win"; rather it is about reconciling a vision of a just and fair world with the reality of oppression and injustice. Teachers with this understanding recognize social change as an ongoing struggle that will not be realized within their lifetime.

In addition to the CIP teachers' misunderstanding of how change happens, they were also still developing their political analysis of injustice. They recognized the symptoms of injustice (i.e. unequal wages, discrimination, lack of healthcare), but they were still learning about the systems in place that maintain oppression. Because of their awareness of the symptoms and not the root causes of inequality, it would follow that their strategies would be to teach and raise awareness about the issues with which they were familiar. However, focusing on the symptoms kept them trapped in a cycle of teaching about injustice without ever addressing the causes of it. At this rate, they were unable to actually create change on the issues that they taught and cared about.

This combination of wanting a "big win" and not having a strong political analysis of the root causes of injustice put them at an impasse and this is when they started to use the Tools of Inaction. They used the tools because they were defensive, similar to the ways in which the teachers in Chapter 2 were defensive when they used the Tools of Whiteness. The tools were different and used for different reasons, but similar nonetheless in that they were employed when the teachers had a sense that they *should* be doing something in addition to what they were already doing and they wanted to justify their inaction. The CIP teachers had a sense that there was another level of action they should aspire to, but they were unsure about how to get there and were overwhelmed by the growing sense that it was going to take more of a commitment than the ones they had already made.

At this point, the CIP teachers faced a crossroads and needed to make a decision. One option could be to lay down the Tools of Inaction by furthering their political analysis about how injustice operates. This would require them to recognize that fighting social injustice consists of many small wins and losses, and accept it, as the teachers in the next chapter do, as a lifetime commitment. On the other hand, they could also go into denial, believing that they have "fixed" injustice by teaching about it and refusing to recognize the pervasive nature of oppression. This option of continuing to use the Tools of Inaction, however, could prove to be emotionally difficult. Because the CIPers were committed to teaching about social injustice, they would have to deal with the contradictory message of their curriculum. On the one hand, they were encouraging their students to take a stand against things they believe are wrong. On the other, the teachers were aware that they were not "practicing what they teach", which would eventually cause discomfort and guilt as they realized the hypocritical nature of their message. At some point, this could either push them toward action, or cause them to retreat from teaching about social issues altogether because of the discomfort it causes for them.

To keep from falling into the trap of never creating actual change, the next step for teachers like those in CIP is to develop their own vision of a more socially just world and work to take steps to realize that vision. A vision of an alternative society provides a destination and an analysis of the forces functions as a map to know how to get there. Without this vision and analysis, teachers committed to social justice remain immobile in their classroom, unable to transform the conditions that they teach about. In contrast, fully realized teachers have both a destination and a map in hand on their journey to reconcile the world they want with the injustice they see. The ways in which these teacher activists enact this both inside and outside the classroom are the basis of the next chapter.

5

RECONCILING THE VISION

Taking Action for Educational Justice

Many teachers, like the ones in the last chapter, do not have a detailed vision of a socially just world that could serve to motivate potential action for liberatory change. This lack of vision, coupled with a limited political analysis of inequality, makes it challenging for such teachers to know how to act for justice, even when they wanted to. As a result, emerging social justice educators may take action here or there or teach about disconnected social issues without a broader agenda for change. Without a coherent vision to drive consistent motivated action, teachers at this stage of political consciousness often find it challenging to know how to move forward as activists inside or outside of their classrooms.

As a member of the New York Collective of Radical Educators (NYCoRE) and a founding member of a national network of similar organizations called Teacher Activist Groups (TAG), I work every day with committed teacher activists locally and across the country. To learn more about how teacher activists define and enact their work, I interviewed ten classroom teachers who were involved in grassroots activism on issues of educational justice. Five of the interviewees were involved in NYCoRE and the other five were activists in Philadelphia (2), Tucson (1), and Milwaukee (2). I interviewed both White teachers and teachers of Color who had a range of teaching experience (2–16 years) in both primary and secondary public schools. This chapter shares how these teacher activists enacted these three commitments in practice and then looks in detail at two cases in action in battles for educational justice that received national coverage in 2011: the right for ethnic studies in Tucson, Arizona, and the struggle for union rights in Wisconsin.

The teacher activists highlighted in this chapter worked hard to "practice what they teach." In enacting their work, teacher activists appear to make three clear commitments, backed by particular practices. The first commitment, "Reconciling the Vision," was to hold a vision of a socially just world and to consistently work to reconcile this vision with the realities of inequality that they saw in the world around them. They attempted to reconcile the contradiction between the world they wanted and the world they were experiencing in the very two ways that the CIP teachers in the last chapter did not. Part of what drove this commitment of reconciliation was the fact that these teacher activists believed that education can be both liberatory and oppressive at the same time. The teacher activists made these commitments on two levels to address both the liberatory and oppressive nature of schooling: "Moving toward Liberation" and "Standing up to Oppression."

The second commitment, "Moving toward Liberation," was enacted in their role as classroom teachers. Within the classroom, teacher activists' ultimate goal was to get students to be conscious, active participants in the world. To do so, they taught their students to think critically, particularly about their communities and broader society. These teachers took a backseat to their students, seeing themselves more as tools or architects, so that their students could take the leading role. To help students develop as people, the teachers valued what their students brought to the classroom and taught their students about the diversity of who they were and the social issues they faced. Such pedagogy allowed the students to understand injustice and have the skills and motivation to do something about it.

Rather than rely on their students to take action alone, the teacher activists in this chapter felt compelled to work to create change themselves because they saw the connection between unjust educational policy and what was happening in their own classrooms. They made a third commitment, "Standing up to Oppression," in which they engaged in ongoing and collective action to rally against the ways that schooling reproduces existing inequalities and maintains the status quo. In their view, to engage in liberatory pedagogy inside of the classroom without fighting injustice outside of it would be inadequate in reconciling their vision of the world they wish to see. Understanding that this was a battle too big to take on alone, the teacher activists chose to work collectively with other teachers, students, families, and communities, and they also worked to get teachers' voices into policy decisions.

Reconciling the Vision: Another World Is Possible

The teacher activists profiled in this chapter were all driven to social justice activism because of their unquenchable desire to reconcile their vision of a more just world with the reality of the injustices they saw in their schools and broader society. In contrast to the emerging social justice educators of the last chapter who used the Tools of Inaction to diminish the discomfort of their own complacency, these teacher activists embraced the contradictions between their vision of social justice and the reality of public schooling in the United States. They used this discomfort as a motivating force for action.

These teachers held a vision of an alternative, more socially just world, and they saw it as a fundamental part of their role as educators to take action to move toward that vision. In defining her teacher activism, Anya, a ninth-grade teacher in Philadelphia, expressed that "I wake up in the morning and I believe that the world can be better and that's why I do the work that I do. [Teacher activism] is founded in the belief that the systems and structures and the ways in which people relate to each other doesn't have to be the only way." Anya, like other activists, believed that "another world is possible" (US Social Forum, 2010) and saw moving society in that direction as part of her role and responsibility as a teacher.

Even though the teachers recognized the possibility that another world was possible, they were realistic. As Ella, a New York City high school math teacher, put it, "It's not like we're gonna win and then I'll be done." Teacher activists such as Ella felt a strong pull to take action to move things toward their vision. Ella, who was only in her third year of teaching, continued: "There are forces in play that are pushing things in a direction that I don't want to see them go, and I just want to be a part of whatever's pushing things in the direction that I do want to go, and it will never be over." Unlike the emerging social justice teachers of the last chapter, these teacher activists had a strong sense of efficacy and saw the reconciliation between the world as it was, and the world as it could potentially be, as a driving force and fundamental part of their role as teachers.

This driving force was so intense that the teachers used terms to describe their need to take action as more of a calling than a choice or activity. In explaining his education activism, Salvador, a high school teacher of Chican@/Latin@ Literature in Tucson, Arizona expressed, "It's like I have to do this, it's not a choice." A surprising number of the teachers interviewed echoed Anya's idea that participating in activism is why they wake up in the morning, demonstrating how integral this work was to their conception of the role of a teacher. Ella expressed that "I couldn't wake up every morning and feel good about the work that I'm doing as a teacher if I wasn't trying to be a part of the struggle against the things that are having a detrimental effect on what education is." Like Ella, these teachers felt that they couldn't feel "good" about their teaching if their work was relegated only to the classroom. They saw it as their calling to reconcile their own visions with the reality of what was happening in the world around them.

Part of what drove this calling was the fact that these teacher activists had a sophisticated political analysis centered on the idea that education can be both liberatory and oppressive at the same time. Rather than acknowledging one of these functions and ignoring the other, they worked on two levels to address both the liberatory and oppressive nature of schooling. First, as classroom teachers, they worked toward their vision of liberation by creating classroom spaces in which students could develop mindsets and skills to take action on issues that affect students' lives. Second, as activists, they organized collectively to rally against the ways in which schooling is set up to reproduce existing inequalities and maintain the status quo. They saw both components of their work as activism: the traditional activism of protesting and organizing, but also the creation of programs and events that build upon the liberating potential of education. As fully realized teacher activists, to engage in liberatory pedagogy inside of the classroom without fighting injustice outside of it would be inadequate in moving toward the world they wish to see.

Moving toward Liberation: Preparing and Supporting Students to Change the World

As classroom teachers, the teacher activists saw it as their role to prepare and support their students to develop both the mindsets and skillsets needed to take action to create liberatory change. Because they saw the future of the movement for social justice as one that will be youth-led, these teacher activists held their students to the same high standards that they held themselves. The teachers believed that their students should take action to make the world closer to the one the students envision. Using similar language to describe his own reasons for why he became a teacher activist, Ray, a third-grade dual-language teacher in New York City, shared what he does in the classroom:

> It means teaching them [students] about the world as it is and how they can be part of changing the world to be more the way … they would want the world to be. [Teaching students] to think about their situation in the world and their experiences and their family's experiences and what's right about that and what's wrong about that and how those things can be changed and how they have been changed historically.

Ray defined his teaching around providing students with the ability to critically analyze their lives in order to create social change. This belief, that the ultimate purpose of education is to prepare students to be critical participants who shape their own lives, sets teacher activists such as Ray apart from traditional educators, who see their main function as passing on knowledge (which will be tested on a high-stakes exam).

Unlike the teachers in Chapter 4, these teachers actually engage in activism in their own lives. Because of this, they have the knowledge and skills to prepare their students to work toward change because they have experience doing it themselves. Ray explained how he was able to bridge his classroom and activism in one particular project in which students organized for the rights of domestic workers. In this project, Ray brought in a guest speaker he knew from his personal activist work who was an organizer working on a bill of rights for nannies and domestic workers. She invited the class to a protest that her organization was holding at city hall.

Held on a Sunday, Ray, four of his students, and their families attended the rally. One of his students, an immigrant from El Salvador whose mother was a domestic worker, was so inspired by the speakers that she asked Ray if she could speak on the stage. Ray immediately spoke to the lead organizer to make the arrangements and helped his student quickly prepare something to say. He recounted:

She had written this little speech and she got up there in front of 200 people and the cameras and the microphones, and she spoke and she was amazing! She nailed it! And she talked about how her mother was broke and how it's not fair and you have to give people more money. And this is an 8-year-old! Afterwards, she was crying and her mother was crying. What was particularly cool was that a radio station was there recording it, and it was on the radio, and we played it for the class who got to hear their classmate speaking at this rally. It was powerful.

Unlike some of the teachers in Chapter 4 who didn't have faith in their students' ability to participate in social change, Ray wasn't worried about whether or not his student "got it." Because of his faith in his student, even when she was not prepared with a speech in advance, he was able to create this powerful opportunity for her to voice her deep understanding of social justice.

Additionally, because Ray had the connections, knowledge, and skills of an organizer, he was able to create the opportunity for this incredible moment of a student taking action about an issue that she faced in her own life that then fed that back into his classroom teaching. "Because I'm an activist, I'm connected to organizations that do work outside of the classroom." Ray explained how his role as an activist supported this work: "So I was able to make that bridge and bring in the organizations from the outside to talk to students. And because I'm comfortable going to rallies and I feel safe taking children to rallies … I was able to reassure parents that this was perfectly safe and that this was gonna be powerful for the children."

Supporting students to be able to take a stand for justice in this way shaped the classrooms of other teacher activists as well: their pedagogy, their behavior in the classroom, the way they engage with their students, and the content that they teach. To prepare and support students to work toward creating a more just world, teacher activists work hard to prepare students to be critical thinkers, particularly about their own lives. They see the ability to think critically as a tool that can help their students have access to more opportunities than society may position them for. As Caroline, a second-grade bilingual teacher in New York explains, "If I can prepare my students to think critically and solve problems and take that approach to learning, they'll be much more successful than if … all they ever learn is how to follow procedures." She believes that it was better to teach her students to understand concepts, rather than simply follow directions, because, "if you only know how to follow a process, then you can only follow your boss's directions." Even as an elementary school teacher, Caroline believes that the way she prepares her students to think at this early age will have a direct impact on their future opportunities for access, independence, and success.

While learning for understanding and critical thinking were goals of the teachers, one particular form of critical thinking characterizes the classrooms of these teacher activists—preparing students to question the world around them. Teacher activists have a sophisticated political analysis about what shapes and maintains inequality, and this helps them to know how to take action for positive change. Because they want their students to also take action, the teachers spend time helping students learn to ask questions to better understand the world so that the students too can develop a political analysis.

Rose, a second-year special education elementary school teacher in Brooklyn, NY, taught a lesson on budget cuts that provides an example of teaching students to question their world. Rose, along with other teachers and parents, was organizing a series of rallies called Fight Back Fridays that would be held at her school along with other schools across New York City. To involve her students, she helped them to question the impact that school closings and unequal resources had on students in different schools. She asked her third graders to think about schools without art classes or enough teachers. "'How do you think the students are doing at those schools?' and they were like, 'They're probably not that happy.'" Building on her students' sense of empathy, she explained to them that those schools were slated to get shut down, "And they were outraged!" She took this moment to teach them about different ways of voicing their opinions, including rallies. She told them, "'You can march around and let everyone know how much we love our school and how important public schools are.' And they were like, 'YEAAAHHHH!!!' They came back to school the next day and a whole bunch of them made signs at home with their parents!" By helping her students question their own school experiences along with the experiences of other schools, and connect those experiences to current issues in education, Rose was able to help her young students start to see how broader issues of funding affect schools. Rather than allow her students to wallow in injustice, she built on their new critical awareness that resulted from questioning what happens when schools don't have funds and provided them with an avenue to take action in coalition with their families and other teachers.

Jai Lia, a first-grade teacher in Milwaukee, Wisconsin, explained the way she enacts critical questioning. She defined it as "being able to guide students to question the things that are being taught to them, and then being able to think what it is that they're hearing or the information they are being given and create an opinion of their own." Jai Lia believes students should not take information for granted, but should be able to critically analyze it. She continued: "Then [students can] connect it to the larger world around them and see what is wrong, what is right, what is justice, what is injustice, what is equality, what is inequality." For Jai Lia and the other teacher activists, their teaching of critical questioning of information helps their students to develop a political analysis of the world around them, which in turn will help them to take action for justice.

To create the liberatory environment in which this kind of critical questioning could be taught, the teacher activists all positioned themselves in the back seat with respect to their students. Unlike traditional teacher-centered classrooms that use a banking model (Freire, 1970) in which the teacher pours information into passive students' brains, these teachers all described themselves using metaphors that demonstrated how they saw their role as one that supports students to embark on their own path of self-discovery. The teachers described themselves as "being a tool that students can use to obtain things," "architects of processes," "fellow people along with their students," "facilitators," and "guides that follow the child." They saw the students as the directors of learning, and their own role was to be there to support that journey as best they could.

This reversal of who directs much of the action in the classroom is also part of the teachers' strategies to prepare independent leaders who know how to find the information they need to take action. Rose explained, "Being able to check my own intentions for how things happen in the classroom and respond to what my students are up for and excited about is a really big thing [in her teaching]." In such classrooms, teaching and learning is driven by students' interests as well as by an understanding of where students are academically and developmentally.

The teachers are willing and able to give up some of the traditional "control" of their classrooms because they deeply value who their students are and what they bring to the classroom. They don't see their students as empty vessels waiting to be filled, but believe that students come with knowledge that can be further developed. Salvador describes this relationship: "A teacher is the person that can and that must acknowledge and value and love who the students are as they enter your room and respect where they want to go and help them formulate those ideas of where they want to go." Rather than taking the leading role of standing in the front of the classroom and dictating what students should know and be able to do, teacher activists like Salvador see themselves as supporting players who help students follow their own dreams.

Teacher activists value the knowledge that students bring with them and use that to shape their classrooms. Rose explains how she does this: "I think [giving] student choice[s] and giving space for my students to share, voice their opinions. Always considering what they bring is a way of stopping the presumption that kids are inexperienced and they don't know anything about the world." Because they see students as people with knowledge and skills, they are able to take a step back, opening the possibility for a different kind of classroom in which students practice the kind of agentic leadership the teacher activists are preparing them for.

Another way that teachers value who students are and what they bring is to create curriculum around the cultural diversity of their classes. As Rose says, "A way of being a teacher activist … is having a really culturally diverse classroom where the cultures that my students bring into the classroom are not only recognized, appreciated, and respected but actually a point of conversation and a point of study." By creating space in their curriculum to discuss topics untouched by teachers such as those in Chapter 2, teacher activists prepare the students to appreciate and respect diversity so that they don't reproduce stereotypes and assumptions about people different from themselves.

Taking this idea one step further, the teacher activists combined teaching about students' lived experiences with critical thinking skills. For Joy, a ninth-grade world history teacher in Philadelphia, this took shape in a six-week unit on the school-to-prison pipeline. She started by connecting to students' lived experiences by asking how many of them knew two to three people in prison. She wanted her students to move past some of the blaming of individuals she had noticed them doing to help them see how systems reproduce and influence the decisions people make. She described some of the activities: "We had adults who were incarcerated as youth come in and speak to us, and we read a comic strip about the prison/industrial complex. Then we tied that to the fact that we're building two new prisons in Pennsylvania and losing ... $650 million in school cuts." Students discussed the priorities of the state represented in these spending patterns and, in culmination, the students signed a petition to get more money in schools rather than in prisons.

Anya, who teaches the same students but in English class, built on the critical consciousness students gained during this unit in Joy's social studies class to further these connections.

> Ninth graders in ten minutes were able to come up to the white board and connect the dots between what's gonna happen next year when we have increased class sizes and decreased amount of teachers. Just that alone [was impressive]. They were able to trace that to how students get pushed out of schools, and then connect that to the school-to-prison pipeline, and then say that the state of Pennsylvania in its priorities is trying to, by design, not to educate them, so that they will end up in prison because it makes somebody money.

Teacher activists such as Joy and Anya start with issues affecting students, then provide them with opportunities to understand how their conditions are shaped by socio-economic forces. Their unit, as is often the case with teacher activists, culminated in students organizing their own action, in this case the students participated in a march for education in DC. Such teachers focus on diversity and social issues within their schools, providing students with practice in questioning and understanding how these issues play out in their own lives, so that they can take action.

In keeping with valuing who students are, teacher activists additionally see it as their role to support students' personal development. The teachers recognize that the life challenges that students face because of systems of oppression affect their social and emotional development, and do what they can to support their students because of and in spite of this. As Joy said, "There is so much going on in their lives that run counter to pure, open development," so, as a response, teachers need to work to provide their students with alternative messages about who they are. Salvador describes this: "My students never had the inspiration to think of an academic identity or space that is fully theirs. So a lot of times [my role] is resuscitating the hope in them to believe in themselves, believe in education, in learning and then they can start loving it." The teachers take on this role because they understand that students' self-image is in part shaped by internalized messages of oppression, and they do what they can to provide a counter-narrative to this so that students can take the lead in the classroom and the broader society.

Teacher activists believe that attending to this personal development prepares students to have the necessary qualities to be social justice change agents. Ray explains how he thinks about this as an elementary school teacher. "You are a model for little people. The way that you treat them and the way you treat their parents, you model the kind of citizen you want to see in the world. You are teaching them to be people." By "people" Ray references a particular kind of person—one who is able to respect others, question the world around them, and work to create change.

Rose also connected the dots between personal relationships, questioning the world around them, and active citizenship: "My ultimate goal is to have my teacher identity be based on developing personal relationships with my students and using those relationships to venture out into the world and try to better our under-standing of each other's lives and other people's experiences and what it means for us to be citizens here." By developing authentic relationships with their students that aren't bound by the classroom door, teacher activists act in solidarity with students. Students become supported to take action because their teachers are standing beside them.

By creating classroom spaces in which students are positioned as active partici-pants whose lives are valued, teacher activists prepare their students to question and act upon the world. What separates these teachers from other social justice educa-tors, similar to the ones in Chapter 4, is that they are not content to depend on the students alone to take action. Instead, driven by their political analysis and sense of duty, these teachers demand of themselves what they hope for their students—to stand up to injustice in order to create a new world. In Anya's words, "We can't just rely on student activism, we have to be bold!"

Standing up to Oppression: Teachers Being Bold!

Unlike the teachers in Chapter 4 who were stuck in indecision, the teachers in this study had a laser-sharp sense that if you see something that is wrong in the world, then you do something about it. As Susan, a pre-school teacher at a public Montessori school in Milwaukee, explained teacher activism: "You make a commitment that wherever you are or whatever you do, if you see something that's not right, that you're going to speak out, not only speak out, but work to make things better and more equitable." The teachers felt a passionate need to take action in the face of injustice. Salvador reinforced this. Referring to his shoes, he said, "You gotta put your puppies on the ground and get to work! ... We should be doing the people's work and really putting our hands in the pot, stirring the masa. If you see something, you have to walk your talk!" Salvador saw this calling for teachers to walk the talk as his responsibility as part of a legacy: "It's our turn to hold the torch. You have to if you really love your kids, your community and believe in folks like César and

Dolores and Gandhi and King and Malcolm, then there is no other way." Each of the teacher activists acted this way on many issues they saw as unjust, from anti-war organizing to queer activism, but the place where they all came together was carrying the torch to interrupt the oppressive nature of education.

Because the teacher activists went into the profession to provide students with high-quality, equal education, they saw it as part of their role to work against forces that were blocking this from happening. Jai Lia expressed that she was called to teach "to be with children and do what is right for them, to pass on knowledge, to protect them and keep them safe." Unlike many teachers, however, she had a broader definition of what it meant to enact this. "You have to be proactive about that and not just do what you're being told to do, not just teaching the curriculum that you're given. So to be an activist for me is to teach, but also ensure that students have a quality education that is fair—making sure they have what they need." It is this broader definition of the dual nature of teaching that includes fighting for students' needs outside of the classroom that sets these teachers apart from the emerging social justice educators of Chapter 4 who confined their roles to issues of curriculum and instruction.

These teacher activists' political analysis was shaped by an awareness of the impact that societal injustice was having on their work inside the classroom. They saw a connection between how outside policies limited the potential for liberatory work inside their classrooms and saw it as part of their role to interrupt this outside the classroom door. Ray explained: "As soon as I got into teaching, I recognized the way that education policy and the larger forces of capitalism affect what goes on in the classrooms. It became clear to me that I couldn't just teach and expect the world to get better, I had to be involved in changing the way that education works in society." Because Ray could connect the dots between the larger political economic context and policies that were being implemented at the school level, he was in a better position than other teachers to take action that could lead to actual change.

Rather than sit idly by or complain about policies that impact the classroom, this analysis helped the teacher activists to know how to take action. Ray continued: "I see on the ground on the job the effects of the policies that I might want to change. If I'm organizing against testing, it's because I see in my classroom how that effects my students, my job, and my school." The policies that impacted his classroom became the targets for Ray and other teacher activists as they decided what they would fight against. The issue of high-stakes testing was in fact the motivating force for Ray to initially become an active member of NYCoRE and he led a working group called "Justice Not Just-Tests" that spoke out at the Mayor's educational policy meetings, and organized many actions against the related issue of merit pay. Unlike the teachers newer to SJE who felt "overwhelmed" and unsure about what to take action on, these teacher activists applied their political analysis about what happened "on the job" to their activism.

The teacher activists had two main approaches for standing up to make education more fair in the face of oppressive forces: 1) by working collectively in groups and

2) by getting teachers' voices into the policy arena. The teacher activists felt that these two strategies were necessary to help them have the broader impact that they saw as critical for making meaningful change.

All of the teachers in this chapter felt it was necessary for their sustainability as activists, and for the strength of their impact, to work with others around issues of educational justice. All of the interviewees were members of grassroots groups of like-minded teachers and they felt that this provided them with knowledge, motivation, strength, a sense of accountability, and the ability to keep going in the face of adversity. Working with allies helped the teachers feel grounded, which was particularly helpful since their viewpoints differed from the mainstream. Jai Lia, who was a member of a number of groups including Educators' Network for Social Justice in Milwaukee, explained that being with like-minded people changed how she connected to teacher activism. "[It] becomes a part of who you are and it becomes a part of your 'normal.' I think sometimes people see activists as really 'out there' and always going against the grain. But when you're with this group of people, it's like why wouldn't you be doing this stuff. This is the work that we do." Rather than always feeling like an outsider, working in a group of allies helped teacher activists "normalize" their stance and their work.

Another major benefit of working in collective groups was the ability to have a broader impact on injustice than if they remained isolated in their classrooms. Ella explained:

> I don't think that individual teachers can just struggle alone in their own classroom and be like "Oh well, that's the system I'm living in so I'll just make the best of it." I think unless we're struggling with the larger issues that make it so our classroom is not as productive of an environment for students as it could be, then well, I don't see the point in teaching. ... I feel like I have to be involved in the struggle for change ... by being connected to movements that are going on that need more people working in them.

Teacher activists understood that they had to fight against the isolating nature of teaching by joining in movements for social change and that this fight was too big to be taken on alone. It was for these reasons that Ella organized with both NYCoRE and the Grassroots Education Movement (GEM). She became a columnist for a progressive education blog, helped create a film called *The Inconvenient Truth behind Waiting for Superman* with GEM, and started a "New Teacher Underground" summer series to support new and alternatively certified teachers to develop a political agenda about teaching in New York. Not knowing what actions would ultimately have the greatest impact, she wanted to play a role in several. Unlike the teachers in the previous chapter whose sense of being overwhelmed by injustice caused them to be inactive, Ella stepped up to organize against injustice from multiple angles.

The other major goal of teacher activists was to fight against the marginalization of teachers by getting their voices into the mainstream and into policy arenas.

Caroline stressed that "Teacher voices are totally eliminated from any discussion. ... The main thing about being a teacher activist is to get teachers' voices out there because teachers can bring so much to the discussion." Echoing the popular marching chant that says "Nothing about Us without Us," Caroline and others felt that because teachers are well versed and experienced in their profession, they should be part of decision-making processes that affect their jobs and their students. Individually, she regularly wrote letters to policy makers and newspaper editors expressing her perspective on educational issues as a classroom teacher.

Through NYCoRE, Caroline multiplied the power of such letters by working collectively. In a remarkable display of principle over self-interest, she and a group of new teachers became involved in the fight for seniority teacher rights in New York City. She fought the ending of a policy called "Last in First out" (LIFO), which held that the last teachers hired would be the first fired in times of budget cuts. The mayor was attempting to end this policy, claiming that often the newest teachers were more qualified than veteran teachers. If he succeeded, Caroline's job would have been more likely to have been protected in the face of looming teacher lay-offs. Instead of saving her job and standing with the mayor, Caroline and her peers saw the dismantling of LIFO as an attack on union rights and an unjust attempt to fire more expensive teachers, which would ultimately harm students. Together these new teachers wrote a letter in support of veteran teachers' rights, sent it to the media and the union, and spoke at a city-wide press conference demanding that seniority rights stay in place.

Jai Lia shared another example of how she and fellow activists worked collectively to get teachers' voices into a policy decision regarding textbook adoptions in Milwaukee. In one of the first actions in which she participated, she joined other teacher activists who had been organizing against a textbook that was about to be adopted that they deemed to be ethnocentric and racist. The teachers invited her to speak at a school board meeting to share her prior experiences as a teacher in New York where she didn't have to use one single textbook, but rather was free to use multiple resources. She told the school board, "If we really are looking to get our children to increase their reading levels or become more critical thinkers, we need to start thinking outside the box and not just depend on this little textbook." After her social studies task force won this battle and successfully recommended a different curriculum, which was eventually adopted, Jai Lia started regularly attending and often speaking at board meetings as a way to continue to insert teachers' voices into policy decisions.

Anya, in agreement with this collective action in policy arenas, reasoned, "Let's have all of us talk together about what we really want [in education policy] and go to the people making the decisions and ask them 'Could there be a more creative way of doing this, is there another way that makes the most sense for what all of the people here need and deserve and demand?'" At the end of Anya's quote she alluded to the sense that teachers need to act in coalition with other key stakeholders, or "all of the people here." She added, "We have to influence the strength of teachers in policy levels and school level decisions and we have to do that through working with students and parents and teachers." By working in coalition with all stakeholders in education, teacher activists demand to have their voices heard in educational policy in order to push against oppressive forces in education.

For the remainder of this chapter, I will focus on two examples of teacher activists who reconciled their vision of justice by simultaneously working toward liberation and against oppression by describing some specific work in which they are involved. In previous chapters, I looked at the teachers as a group and focused on trends that represented their journey. As the teacher activists in this chapter are working to enact the commitments of teacher activism, I have chosen to look in more detail at two specific cases because they serve as examples that typify the attitudes and behaviors of teachers who practice what they teach. Looking more closely at what these teacher activists are actually doing on the ground provides us with models of what is possible when teachers reconcile their visions of justice inside and outside of the classroom. Additionally, these two examples garnered a great deal of media attention and both illustrate the ways in which these educators actualize their definitions of teacher activism.

The first example focuses on the work of Jai Lia Lee and Susan Lehrer, two teacher activists in Milwaukee, Wisconsin, who worked tirelessly to battle their governors' attack on public workers and unions that began during the 2010–11 school year. The second example describes the work of Salvador Villa, a high school teacher in Tucson, Arizona, and his battle to defend the Mexican American Studies program in which he teaches. His program was deemed "illegal" by the state of Arizona for allegedly "promoting the overthrow of the American government" and he and his fellow teachers filed a lawsuit against the state.

Standing up for Worker Rights in Wisconsin

Jai Lia Lee and Susan Lehrer, a first-grade and early childhood teacher respectively, are both members of the teacher activist group Educators' Network for Social Justice (ENSJ) in Milwaukee, Wisconsin. They are both active in their local union and other city-wide efforts for educational justice. In February of 2011, they learned of a budget repair bill that their governor, Scott Walker, had introduced that would take away collective bargaining rights for most public workers, including teachers. Jai Lia and Susan's response and subsequent actions helped to contribute to a series of protests in the state capital over several weeks that drew daily crowds of 13,000–100,000 protesters (Bauer & Richmond, 2011; FoxNews.com, 2011; NOLA.com, 2011; Sewell, 2011).

For Susan, who was raised by union activist parents and who had been involved within her local union, the Milwaukee Teachers' Education Association (MTEA), the news of the Scott Walker bill came as a shock. She learned the details of the bill over public radio as she cleaned her classroom on a Friday afternoon after school. Walker's bill included severely limiting collective bargaining for public employees, meaning that public workers such as teachers would have no say over their rights such as healthcare, discipline procedures, sick leave, and other work rules (Stein & Marley, 2011). Workers would also have to pay double their current premiums into their health benefits and increase their payment to their pensions, decreasing their take-home pay by 8 percent (Huttleston, 2011). Along with many other components, the bill would end seniority protection while also cutting state funding to local school districts, forcing lay-offs that put more experienced (read: expensive) teachers at risk.

Unlike other teachers who might just sigh and think such a bill was an outrage, but one that was out of their control, Susan immediately felt the need to talk to other colleagues about it. "I was like, I can't believe this is happening! And I ran to another teacher in the hallway and I said, 'Oh my God, do you know what I just heard on the radio?' And I told her and we were just shocked. We didn't quite know what to say or do at that point. It was just like okay, now we're just gonna go home." While she initially had the dejected response of most people faced with what felt like a wall of injustice, it only took a few hours for that initial sense of defeat to transform to resistance. Rather than stay at home, Susan felt the need to reconcile her vision for justice with this attack on unions and public workers, and began to push back against this bill. In keeping with the commitment of teacher activists to stand up to injustice, Susan, Jai Lia, and other teacher activists began organizing over email and making phone calls.

Susan, who previously expressed that she had made a commitment as an activist to do something in the face of injustice, worked to enact this ideal by calling upon other teachers to organize a city-wide sick-out of Milwaukee public school teachers. By that Sunday, Susan and Jai Lia were at the state union's office making phone calls to talk about the bill with other teachers and to try to get them to go to Madison, the capital, to protest. She explained why she went. "It's kind of like when people face a tragedy, you always think that you just want to do something. Somehow that's kind of a coping mechanism. If I can do something, then I'll feel a little better about this." While the emerging social justice educators in Chapter 4 chose not to act when they faced issues of injustice—such as being threatened with pink slips—Susan had the opposite reaction. As a teacher activist, she felt the need to reconcile reality with justice and found solace in taking action. Within just a few days, their collaborative efforts within ENSJ and other groups mobilized over 1000 people to protest in front of Walker's Milwaukee County residence.

Despite the fact that this activism required some level of risk, Susan and Jai Lia felt called to act so that they could reconcile their vision of education with the attacks they and their fellow teachers faced. Susan reflected on the escalation of the kind of actions she was organizing. "There's the kind of activism that you could do in a comfortable place, like it's relatively easy to go to a school board meeting and state your testimony. It's another thing to think, okay, I've gotta skip school tomorrow and I could get in trouble for this." Susan knew that it was taking it to a new level and moving "outside the comfort zone" to not only put herself on the line by calling out sick to go to the capital, but to also ask other teachers to take a similar risk. Susan's drive to action was stronger than her need to protect herself and her job and she saw the need to organize as a test of her commitment. She continued, "I mean in a sense those tests are good because it's reassuring your commitment in general to the cause."

Jai Lia, like Susan, enacted the commitment of teacher activism to stand up to injustice by calling out sick and going to Madison in a show of solidarity with workers across the state. She recounted:

> The people that I am connected with through ENSJ and through these different groups, we started talking like we gotta go. This is really important—this is huge! We need to go and we need to be on that line and we need to be fighting for our rights! It started to become a really scary thing, but I called up my friends and said, "Let's go."

Despite the fact that their local superintendent and local union president had not supported a sick-out so that Milwaukee teachers could go to Madison, these teacher activists prioritized their calling for justice, rather than the instructions of their bosses.

For Jai Lia, going to Madison on Wednesday was a transformational experience as a teacher activist because of the strength and energy of the united collective of attendees. Jai Lia described her first day in Madison: "In terms of activism, I really didn't feel like an activist until I was actually there and being surrounded by these people who were angry and fighting for their rights and being so collective and so united! It was amazing! There are no words to express that feeling that I had at that moment." This moment of collective unity transformed the way Jai Lia understood activism. "This is why people march and fight back and do what they need to do. It makes all the protests that you hear about in our history so much more poignant and so much more meaningful." Through taking personal risks to stand up for justice, Jai Lia benefited from the energy and camaraderie of participating in this historic showing of collective action.

Unlike the emerging teacher activists who may, or may not, have chosen to attend such a rally, Jai Lia and Susan had an analysis of how this bill was connected to a broader struggle for educational justice. They agreed with one of the popular slogans during the weeks of protests that said, "Teachers' working conditions are students' learning conditions." Their understanding of this connection between the bill and their classroom caused them to participate in a more consistent and involved manner than simply showing up once or twice after school to a rally or meeting.

Jai Lia and Susan continued to organize relentlessly to get Milwaukee teachers to represent at the capital, calling out several days that week and spending hours making phone calls organizing more and more teachers to do the same. By the hundreds, Milwaukee teachers stood in solidarity with Madison teachers who had already shut down their schools. Over 400 Milwaukee teachers called out sick on

Thursday causing major upsets in the district. In response, the Superintendent demanded that all principals call every teacher that had called out sick and read them a letter explaining that they would face disciplinary action. Regardless, by Friday enough Milwaukee teachers had called out that the Superintendent was forced to cancel school for the day.

Triumphant, both teachers credited the fact that they were surrounded by like-minded allies and that they were working as a group as instrumental in pushing them to keep going to organize the successful sick-out. Susan contended, "A critical factor was that I was surrounded that whole time with other teacher activists that were like 'No, we gotta do this ... now is the time to act.'" Rather than remain alone and isolated, shaking their heads in the face of injustice, Jai Lia and Susan enacted the commitment of teacher activism to work collectively with other teacher activists to create change, increasing both their motivation and their impact.

With the time that has passed since this incident, the Governor's bill was pushed through with questionable tactics and, at the time of writing this book, it has been subsequently held up in litigation. Despite these set-backs, Jai Lia and Susan have remained active in the struggle. Seeing each new challenge not as a loss, but as another opportunity to reconcile their vision with reality, they have continued to fight back against the bill through multiple union, policy, and school-based strategies.

By refusing to give up, these teachers accomplished a number of goals. They modeled resistance to their students who will learn that activists stay in the fight despite set-backs because the goal is to push back against continued attacks, even if there isn't one big "win." These teacher activists' perseverance also contributed to blocking neoliberal reforms that sought to demolish public education. Without people who are willing to stand up to injustice, laws such as Governor Walker's bill would be in place across the country. The impact that teacher activists have is often more far reaching than their local community. In fact, when the governor of New York, Andrew Cuomo, was being pressured to pass the LIFO law ending teacher seniority rights at the same time as the Wisconsin uprising, he made a veiled reference to Madison, saying that it was not a good time to upset labor and backed off, even if momentarily. The work of Susan, Jai Lia, and the other teacher organizers can claim some responsibility for that.

Unlike the teachers in Chapter 4 who didn't have a vision of an alternative, socially just world or a belief in their own ability to contribute to making it happen, teacher activists like Jai Lia and Susan were clear on what they were doing and why they were doing it. They knew that they had to continue, not because they were seeking approval from external sources like the CIPers, but because their drive to actualize the world that they want does not allow them to stop.

Fighting Ethnic Cleansing in Arizona

Salvador Villa, who entered teaching to be a role model for Chicano youth, started working in the then titled "Raza Studies Program" at Tucson High a few years into his teaching career. Born out of struggle, the now titled Mexican American Studies Department (MASD) in Tucson, Arizona, was created by parents, teachers, and community members to improve the educational experiences and outcomes of the areas' Latino students. Boosting an explicit social justice standpoint, MASD is dedicated to culturally relevant pedagogy, with a particular focus on the contributions of Mexican Americans to US history. Not shying away from an explicitly political mission, the MASD model is based on "Critically Compassionate Intellectualism" (Arce, 2010b). As described in their newsletter, "Critically Compassionate Intellectualism combines curriculum (using counter-hegemonic content), pedagogy, and student–teacher interaction (authentic caring) as a model for increased academic achievement for all students, with an emphasis on Latino students in particular and students of color in general" (Arce, 2010b). For a teacher activist like Salvador, who is driven by the teacher activist commitment of creating a liberatory space for students to develop as critical, active participants in a democracy, teaching in MASD turned out to be a perfect fit.

In his pursuit of creating a liberatory space for his students, Salvador enacted critically compassionate intellectualism through the way he interacted with his students to the curricular content that he chose. His literature class included authors from multiple backgrounds, but they all reflected some of the challenges and experiences that his students faced, and Salvador used this as a springboard to help students make decisions about their own lives. For example, when reading Luis Rodriguez's (1994) book *Always Running*, Salvador asked his students to go beyond their initial surface observation that the lead character is "bad" because he sells drugs. Instead, Salvador had his students explore the socio–economic conditions of the 1950s. They looked at the English-only policies the character faced in school and how that caused him as a little boy to pee in the corner because he was too afraid to ask to use the bathroom. The students explored how that experience would shape the character's orientation toward school in the future.

Salvador taught literature this way because he wanted his students to see that policies and conditions shape the choices people make, and he helped them learn to apply this idea to their own lives so they can develop their own political analysis. "We use that as a launch point to talk about our world and experiences of the students." His first assignment at the start of the year, after reading a book about a Spokane Indian child's educational experiences by Sherman Alexie (2007), is to have the students free-write if they have ever felt dehumanized by school.

> Every year, multiple members in the class within one week of being in my classroom are able to already tell how authentic and realistic it'll be in here. They open up and tell horrific stories. It's awful but it's also healing. … It can be used as a launching pad, it's a narrative into all these different types of writing my students need, a narrative and obviously an analysis that we're about to engage upon for either two semesters or four.

As a teacher activist creating a liberatory space, Salvador builds upon students' experiences to help them develop both a political analysis and academic skills such as, in this example, narrative writing.

Another way that Salvador's classroom reflected the characteristics of teacher activism is that Salvador not only tried to develop his students' activist and intellectual spirit, but he is also a model of these qualities himself. Unlike the teachers in Chapter 4, he does not ask the students to do things that he himself is not engaged in:

> They know who I am best from what they see me do, which includes being a doctoral student and what that means as a Chicano. I let them know what that means and then I compare myself as a student to them. Because I want them to grow into their role as a student, but I also want them to grow into their role as an activist ... so they see me at protests, they see me at marches, they see my family.

Salvador models his twin goals for his students, to develop both as scholars and as activists, and these goals were evidenced in his pedagogy in which he linked academic skills to a liberatory pedagogy. He would tell them about current issues and activism he was engaged in, and then used that as the basis of his literacy curriculum. He furthered, "So I tell them ... that I'm communicating with school board members. ... And I'm telling you this," he said to students, "so that you learn about how that world works just as much as you learn how to write a tight paragraph or a great essay." Salvador's pedagogy in which students analyzed literature to make links between policy and lived experiences matched how Salvador taught them about social issues. Unlike the emerging CIP teachers, however, Salvador's actual engagement in social action strengthened his ability to develop those skills in his students. As a model of activism, his students understood that Salvador enacted the philosophy of "practice what you teach." The fact that Salvador was willing to fight for their education served as a model and motivation for his students to do the same.

The students in Salvador's program were able to speak of the impact that the curriculum based on critically compassionate intellectualism had on them, regardless of whether they were Mexican American or not. Adrian Laurenzi, a White MASD alum from the class of 2008, was one of Salvador's former students. He explained the impact that Salvador's classes had on his development as a critical-conscious participant in the world.

> It wasn't until taking Chicano Literature that I began to make progress in how I dealt with the issue of race. Discussing racial issues with other students and analyzing these issues in assigned texts helped me to obtain a more constructive and critical view of race. The writing projects I did for the class were empowering because they provided me with an outlet to devise ideas for solutions to these societal problems. I no longer felt guilty about racial prejudice because I had joined the fight against it. Raza Studies converted my guilt into

motivation for taking action and working to promote social justice continues to be one of my most important life aspirations (Duarte, 2009).

Adrian described the impact of Salvador's reading and writing assignments had on his ability to move past some of his own Tools of Whiteness to be able to promote social justice. Adrian's words validate that Salvador's strategy of linking academic skills to a liberatory pedagogy came to fruition.

In keeping with the teacher activist commitment of creating a liberatory space, Salvador and the other MASD teachers wanted their students to question the world around them, understand how hegemony operates, and take action for positive change. Selena Bush, another alumnus from the program, explained the impact MASD had on her development as a person active in the world: "These classes were instrumental in my development as a human being and as an interested member of my community invested in its growth" (Bush, 2011). Selena felt that MASD was successful in building curriculum based upon who she is and where she comes from, and that the program used that information as a way to help her actively participate in society. Although much of the history discussed in her classes addresses issues such as colonization and other challenges that Mexicans and Chicanos face, she did not experience this as disheartening. Rather she expressed that "learning your history empowers you, especially we who have been so powerless." She did not mince her words in describing the impact of MASD's social justice pedagogy, contending, "Countless students have been saved from dropping out by these classes, because they teach us that we do have a voice, that we do have power, and that what we say matters."

The proof that Salvador and MASD's culturally based, social justice pedagogy is successful for reaching all students, but particularly Chicano students, was backed up by these students' voices, but by traditional data measurements as well. By all conventional measures, particularly the kinds favored by the current neoliberal educational reformers, the program was a success. Students who participated in the MASD program were three times more likely to pass the state tests reading section, four times more likely to pass the writing section, and two and a half times more likely to pass the math section compared with similarly situated students (Arce, 2010a). In fact, compared with the national average graduation rate of 44.0 percent for Mexican Americans, MASD students have a graduation rate of 97.5 percent (Arce, 2010a). More than 67 percent of MASD students in the years between 2004 and 2010 enrolled in post-secondary education after graduation, which is 193 percent greater than the national average of 24 percent for Mexican Americans (Arce, 2010a).

One would think that given the success of the program on both conventional quantitative measures as well as demonstrated by the passionate testimonials of former students, this program that has managed to produce critically conscious college-going alumni that defy demographic statistics would be one that educators and policy makers across the country would be rushing to scale up and replicate. Unfortunately, one would be wrong.

When Salvador and the other MASD teachers prepare students to think critically and understand the hegemonic forces at play in the United States, they are consistently attacked. However, in keeping with the tenets of teacher activism, these attacks were not enough to dissuade Salvador and his colleagues from moving away from their vision of preparing critically conscious students. As Salvador recounted,

> The hate started coming almost immediately at my school, from colleagues that were very much Republican, right-winged folks and so they had their agenda and they went after us. A lot of unseemly things have happened, from hate speech on the door, to personal problems where somebody's calling us a racist, or someone said to a student of ours, "Why are you taking that fake history?"

However, consistent with his philosophy as a teacher activist, Salvador saw each of these battles, from collegial conflicts, to state-sanctioned attacks, as yet another opportunity to reconcile his vision of justice with the reality of the forces pushing against it. "That's part of the game," he reflected, "and in the beginning I was really hurt by it, but now I'm like aiight, that's another moment, let's move on, let's check 'em and move forward." This attitude and passionate desire to create a different world for his students allowed him to move past individual losses because he had his eye on the broader prize of justice.

Unfortunately, Salvador and MASD have had repeated opportunities to test their will to "check 'em and move forward" in the face of increasing attacks on their program. Because MASD was aimed at exposing hegemony and preparing students to take action, the powers that be were intent on putting an end to this form of education. After years of vigilant attempts to shut down the program (Biggers, 2010), then superintendent of Tucson Unified School District (TUSD), Tom Horne, introduced State Bill 2281 to end the Ethnic Studies program, which was signed into law by Governor Jan Brewer on May 11th, 2011 (Pitzi, 2010). Based on Horne's previous allegations of the TUSD program, the bill makes it illegal to have any courses that "1) Promote the overthrow of the United States Government, 2) Promote resentment toward a race or class of people, 3) Are designed primarily for pupils of a particular ethnic group, and 4) Advocate ethnic solidarity instead of the treatment of pupils as individuals" (House Bill 2281, 2010).

Tom Horne, and the bill itself, relies on arguments uncannily similar to the Tools of Whiteness used by the teachers in Chapter 2. Rather than teach about the true history of the realities of people of Color in the United States, Horne relies on Tools of Whiteness to cling to the idea of teaching a "positive" version of history. As he expressed in a debate on CNN when asked if racism still existed, "That's not the predominant atmosphere of America. America's a land of opportunity. And we should be teaching the kids that this is a land of opportunity, and not teach them the 'downer' that they're oppressed and they can't get anywhere" (Cooper, 2010). Like Dawn and other teachers in Chapter 2, Horne reveals his lack of racial consciousness in the assumption that students that learn about a "downer" version of history will cause them to resent the United States, and, most likely, White people.

Horne alleged that MASD is a "race-obsessed philosophy and it's a downer philosophy" in which teachers "divide [students] by race and teach the Black kids Black history, the Chicano kids Chicano history, the Asian kids Asian history" (Cooper, 2010). This flawed understanding of the program is based on a critically unconscious version of the world in which any discussion of race violates principles of individuality and is automatically racist. Additionally, it points to the connection between individual and institutional racism. While Horne and each teacher in Chapter 2 may hold their own hegemonic understandings of racism, as educators and politicians their stances transform from "opinions" to policies that serve to maintain oppression and White supremacy.

As teacher activists who have made a commitment to stand up to injustice, Salvador, his colleagues, and their students refused to sit back against these oppressive forces working to decimate the liberatory space that they and their predecessors had fought to create. Tirelessly they worked, as Salvador explained, "to protect something that has been so transformational and so healing and so life-saving for our students." Salvador, alongside the other teachers in MASD as well as current and former students and other supporters, has organized countless protests, spoken at school board meetings, held press conferences, travelled to other cities and states to fundraise for their cause, participated in the creation of a film about the struggle, circulated petitions, and attempted just about every other tactic possible to defend their program. Never have they used the Tools of Inaction to back down from their sense of responsibility or call to continue the struggle.

Salvador and ten other ethnic studies teachers' filed a lawsuit against Horne, Brewer, and the Arizona state bill. They claimed that HB 2281 is in violation of their first-amendment rights to free speech and their fourteenth-amendment rights of due process and equal protection because they believe the law is specifically aimed at Latinos ('2010 SBA No. 7763,' 2010). Unlike the fantasy of the "lone savior" in Chapter 2, Salvador engaged the teacher activist stance of working collectively in a group with his colleagues with the support of his students and their community.

Salvador and the other supporters continued the fight despite the losses along the way in this struggle to maintain MASD over the last seven years. He described his drive to keep going: "They have come at us and our students for a long, long time and … we can't let them win. Even if they win these little battles, it's gonna hurt like hell, but we gotta win the war for lack of a better saying, but well that's what it feels like, to be honest." Despite losing the "little battles," Salvador and his colleagues continued to work to reconcile their vision of equitable education for their students with the harsh attacks against their program. His eyes remained firmly on the prize. "We gotta win the whole thing, we gotta make sure that law and all those people that trumpeted that law get what … they deserve. And that's justice in their face. Saying 'You can't do this to people, you can't do this to children, you can't do this to anyone. This is wrong.'" Salvador spoke to two commitments of teacher activism, standing up to injustice, while creating a liberatory system of education.

He followed up with the second goal of fighting injustice: "After this [the lawsuit] is over, as long as we create the environment to recreate what we built for another generation, then I'm perfectly cool with that. ... It's about who's on the wall and it's really about what our parents went through and what our grandparents went through." Seeing his work as part of a legacy that is his responsibility to defend and pass on, he exclaimed, "That's what it is to me, it's like I have to do this, it's not a, a choice. Well, that makes it sound bad, like I don't want to. But my 'have to' is a 'want to!' It's a desire to love myself and my family and our history."

Conclusion

The day that I started writing this conclusion, I learned over Facebook that Anya had been given a pink slip by the School District of Philadelphia along with 1500 other teachers. While the lay-offs, part of the broader neoliberal attack on education and all things public, are being contested in court, Anya's teacher activist spirit did not waver. In a blog post just hours after she received the news of her impending unemployment from a career she loves, she wrote:

> Today, I lost my job in the School District of Philadelphia, and the worst part had nothing to do with my paycheck, my 403(b), my health insurance, or the imminent scramble to figure out what to do next. The worst part was the tears streaming down my students' faces when they said: "But we fought! We organized! We went to Harrisburg and DC and the District. We marched and protested and doorknocked. And we lost. The state is still not giving us the money, and we're still losing our teachers. I can't believe we fought so hard, but lost anyway."

Rather than focus on her own personal needs, Anya's focus was on her students and the message they would take away from this loss. After a semester of teaching her students about the city/state budget cuts and providing them with the skills and opportunities they would need to organize against them, she knew it was her continued responsibility to help them through this loss.

Despite her anxiety about her own future, within minutes of the news she remarkably was able to use this set-back as a teachable moment to prepare her students for the realities of organizing. She responded to her students:

> You'll probably lose again. You're going to win and lose countless times. ... If you wake up in the morning and believe that the world can be a better place, then you're an organizer. And you're going to figure out an improved strategy to win. Otherwise, you're just going to have to lay down and watch everything crumble. Is that what you want?

When the students responded that this was not what they wanted, she continued her impromptu lesson on social change, "OK. Then be sad today. That's fine. But tomorrow, you better wake up believing that the world can be transformed. I will be here to help you think through how." Just as Anya tells her students, teacher activism will always be a series of wins and losses, because the drive to action comes not from the hope of one big "win" in which everything is then over, but from an ongoing process of "transforming the world" to more closely match one's vision of justice and liberation. Because of this, the teacher activists in this book are able to keep going in the face of the continued attacks on teachers, students and education, despite losses on individual campaigns.

Like the other educators in this chapter, Anya's pedagogy in the face of injustice demonstrates fully enacted teacher activism and social justice pedagogy. These teachers prepare their students to be critically conscious participants in the world and then work alongside them to stand up for justice, particularly educational justice. Unlike the teachers in Chapter 2 who have no recognition of inequality or the emerging social justice teachers in Chapter 3 and 4 who may teach about social justice issues but don't "practice what they teach," these teacher activists roll up their sleeves and get to work to stand up to injustice when and where they see it. As Joy described, teacher activists work "two full-time jobs" to make the most of the liberatory potential of education while fighting against its reproductive and oppressive tendencies. These educators are motivated not by achieving specific outcomes on individual campaigns, but by reconciling their vision of justice with current realities.

Students need more teachers like the ones in this chapter to provide them with a safe space in which they can both gain access to institutions that traditionally underserve them while also learning tools of resistance (Morrell, 2007). Teacher activists understand the challenges students face because of institutionalized oppression and see it as part of their role to help students deconstruct and transform their contexts. While other teachers may understand some of the challenges, because they don't have a fully formed understanding of what is maintaining inequality, they are less equipped to support students through it. Anya described her role in this sense as being a buffer:

> You have to be the buffer between the oppressive institutions that don't care about young people and make this peaceful little oasis in your classroom where you can be like "come inside, learn and maybe something will inspire you to life and opportunity and not death and incarceration" ... that the system sets them up for.

Without teacher activists helping students negotiate such life choices, students will experience only the injustice of education, without knowing the liberatory potential it holds.

Given that the onslaught of attacks on public education is going to continue, we need more teachers like the ones in this chapter to stand up and join the struggle for educational justice. While a one-time showing of thousands of teachers to an isolated march (i.e. Save our Schools 7/30/11) is a powerful signal of the strength of teachers united, most of the attendees of such events, such as the teachers in Chapter 4, will show up once and go home. What makes the orientation of teacher activists vital for the struggle is that they are willing to continue the fight even in the face of loss because their eyes are on the bigger prize. They recognize that their vision may not be realized in their lifetime, but they see it as their responsibility to do all they can to push back against the forces of oppression, rather than "watch everything crumble."

The development of these components—a political analysis and a vision of justice— is the key difference between the emerging social justice educators and the teacher activists. The emerging social justice educators did not become activists because they didn't have a full understanding of how inequality is maintained, so it was difficult for them to understand how to fight against it. Additionally, without knowing the history of how social movements and social change happen, they felt powerless in the face of injustice. Teacher education can play a role in support of these emerging teachers to develop an analysis and historical knowledge. One way that teacher education can do this is to link pre-service teachers with teacher activist groups such as those that the teacher activists in this chapter participate in.

By creating these links between teacher education and teacher activism, pre-service teachers can be provided with opportunities to not only learn that there are justice-minded educators out there, but to also participate in these broader social movements if they so choose. By participating in teacher activist groups like the ones the teachers in this chapter have created, new educators can move away from the often "apolitical" content of their teacher education classes to learn more about the issues facing schools and communities from the perspective of people in the field. They can see that there are other teachers who make it part of their jobs to work within the system to do what is right for their current students, while working to change the constraints that are perpetuating unjust educational experiences for their future students. Through these connections, pre-service teachers can develop an orientation from the beginning that working outside of the classroom is something to aspire to.

An additional benefit of linking teacher education and teacher activism is that teacher educators can improve their own pedagogy by working side by side with teacher activists. By working together, teacher educators learn more about the ways that unjust educational policy impacts the daily lives of teachers. As a result, they are better able to prepare pre-service teachers to learn to negotiate and challenge the realities of public school teaching in our current context. By being more aware of the ways in which neoliberal reforms play out in real classrooms, teacher educators can also use their academic voices and research to join with teachers, parents, and students as a united front against the lack of democracy and transparency in public education.

In terms of the future of public education, teacher activists are needed to be on the vanguard to be a public left voice to stop the overwhelming pull to the right in an educational reform movement led by corporate interests, bankers, and hedge-fund operators (Gabriel & Medina, 2010). Teacher activists are needed to remind the public that teachers are people that love your children, not greedy people who are milking the system as the media and politicians would have us believe (Bergquist & Stein, 2010). Teacher activists are needed to push the unions out of complacency to fight back against the forces of neoliberal reforms. In Chicago, a teacher activist group, the Caucus for Rank and File Educators (CORE), organized themselves to take over the Chicago Teachers Union and have been able to enact a progressive agenda through the union. Similarly, in Milwaukee, with the help of organizing by Jai Lia and Susan, the leader of their teacher activist group, ENSJ, was elected the head of MTEA, their local union. In other cities, many grassroots education organizations are uniting to attempt a similar strategy. Without these efforts, without the combination of teaching and activism, there would be no consistent, meditated push back to stop the corporatization of schools that serve limited private interests over the public good.

6

"MAKING A DIFFERENCE"

Teaching in the Classroom and Organizing in the Streets

In this book, I argue that teachers who are dedicated to creating a more socially just world need to move beyond integrating social issues into the classroom by also working as activists as part of an ongoing movement for justice. The work of educating students about issues such as racism, poverty, and intolerance is a key component of social justice education that helps children develop empathy and a political analysis at a young age. However, by remaining solely in the classroom, teachers may raise the awareness of their students about particular topics, but will be unable to impact the root causes of issues of injustice that they find problematic. In order to move society from inequality to justice, fully realized teacher activists must practice what they teach by additionally engaging in sustained, ongoing action in coalition with parents, students, and other teachers to battle the forces that stand in the way of justice.

The journey of becoming this type of teacher activist is an ongoing one that can be characterized by certain key stages along the way. As represented by teachers in Chapter 2, many teachers start with oppositional stances toward social justice because of their hegemonic understandings about race and difference. Until oppositional teachers are able to recognize that inequality exists, develop empathy for people who experience marginalization, and begin to fill in some of the gaps of their historical knowledge of inequality, they will continue to hold on to their problematic stances by using Tools of Whiteness to dismiss new knowledge that could potentially move them forward toward social justice education (SJE). If they are unable to move forward, these teachers' roles in schools will be to maintain and perpetuate educational inequality by enacting their problematic stereotypes about the capacity and potential of students different from themselves.

Fortunately, if teachers at this stage are able to recognize inequality, develop empathy, and build historical knowledge, a political analysis can begin to develop that serves to motivate such emerging social justice educators. Armed with the belief that inequality is wrong, teachers at this stage often work to build a liberatory space for their students within their classrooms. By honoring who students are and by creating curriculum that helps them to become aware of social issues, emerging social justice educators want to use education as a vehicle for change. While this critically important work lays the foundation for students to engage in social change, it is not sufficient in impacting the root causes of inequality.

To move to the next stage of becoming teachers who do impact oppression, emerging social justice educators must begin to see that the struggle for social justice is one that requires more time and dedication than the already difficult job of classroom teaching. Rather than constructing activism as a "task" or something to feel guilty about not doing, emerging social justice educators need to develop an orientation toward activism in which they see it as a calling—something they can't imagine *not* doing.

Having developed this sense, fully realized teacher activists wake up in the morning with a mission of working to create a more just world because they would feel incomplete as a teacher if they did not engage in the activist work outside of the classroom. This is because they recognize the dual nature of education. Like the emerging social justice educators, they recognize that education can provide a liberatory space in which students are honored for who they are and encouraged to learn how to envision a just world. While emerging social justice educators do focus on creating this liberatory space, teacher activists add to this work the recognition that education is an institution that reinforces inequality and seek to address schooling's oppressive nature as well. Because teacher activists recognize both the liberatory and reproductive dimensions of education, they feel as though their work inside of the classroom fulfills only half of their responsibilities as a teacher.

What is remarkable about the work of teacher activists is that they keep going even in the face of defeat. Despite the senate bill that decimated teachers' rights in Wisconsin passing, local teacher activists continue to organize. Despite state laws declaring their ethnic studies program illegal, Tucson teacher activists continue to organize. Despite receiving record numbers of pink slips and budget cuts, teacher activists nationally continue to organize. Why do these teachers continue to persist when most of their colleagues shrug their shoulders in defeat?

The teacher activists in this book persist because they are driven by a larger mission than the individual battles that they fight. Unlike emerging social justice educators, the teacher activists have a political analysis of social change that helps them to move beyond individual defeats. They have historical background knowledge that helps them to understand that change is not caused by a "big win" but rather by a series of wins and losses. Ella demonstrates this in discussing the abolition of slavery:

> We have this 20/20 vision of how the abolition of slavery happened, but when you're in it, there's no way to know what exactly it is that will be transformative. Who would've been able to say at that time, "Well, we need to write an anti-slavery book. We'll call it *Uncle Tom's Cabin*. And then we

need Frederick Douglass to have pamphlets." There were hundreds and hundreds and hundreds of other actions going on that had some impact, and, in some cases, didn't have an impact. But who knew? The reality is that, in that time, you didn't know what would end it.[1]

The teacher activists in this book drew on their historical knowledge of how change operates to understand that it takes many tactics, strategies, rallies, and protests in order to build to the events that push change. Ella connected this understanding to her own reasons for persisting and participating in groups such as the New York Collective of Radical Educators (NYCoRE) and Grassroots Education Movement (GEM). "So that's how I feel. I don't know that GEM is gonna be the thing that makes a difference, or NYCoRE is the thing that's gonna makes a difference. All I know is I can't not be doing something." By believing that change happens through multiple efforts, teacher activists continue to persist because they believe that their collective and cumulative efforts will pay off, regardless of what happens with individual actions.

Some may see Ella's statement as unstrategic, but that is not what is going on here. Rather, her sentiments demonstrate why teacher activists don't give up. While teacher activists may be willing to try multiple strategies to try to create change, they are not random or unplanned. Armed with their vision and political analysis, such teachers understand the forces that they are up against. They know what their targets are, and believe that it will take a variety of tactics to push back against it. They know there will not be one big win, but rather multiple small wins and losses over time.

In our current context in which neoliberal forces are decimating public schooling as we know it, we need groups of teacher activists who are willing to persist and struggle despite losses. As Margaret Mead expressed, "Never doubt that a small group of thoughtful, committed citizens can change the world. Indeed, it is the only thing that ever has" (ThinkExist.com Quotations). While this may ring of romanticism, the history of social movements and social change backs this quote up. Ella and other teacher activists use this sentiment as a motivating drive to push back against the forces that are impacting their students and schools.

In this day and age, the costs of not fighting back are too great. The gaps between rich and poor are at the highest they have been since the gilded age (Institute for Policy Studies Programs, 2010). The accumulation of wealth and power at the top of society is playing out in an increasingly two-tiered system of education. With 44 percent of Congress members among the 1 percent of the country's millionaires (Montopoli, 2009), people interested in democracy must begin to question in whose interest most policies, and, in this case, educational policies are being made. Across the country, educational policies are pushing schools to become increasingly separate and unequal (Harvard Graduate School of Education, 2010; Kozol, 2005).

The effects of these policies are playing out nationally. Forty thousand teachers lost their jobs in 2010. Class size in cities such as Detroit is up to 60 students

(Rotherham, 2011). Testing corporations' revenues are in the billions through the expansion of high-stakes testing that drives most curriculum across the country (Lussenhop, 2011; Miner, 2004/2005; Toch, 2006). The results of such tests are used to make punitive educational decisions that disproportionately impact students of Color, resulting in retention and increased dropout rates that subsequently drive the school-to-prison pipeline (FairTest, 2007; Fine, 2003; Haimson, 2003). Arts, sports, and afterschool programs are being slashed across the country. For-profit schools and charter school investors are profiting at the expense of already under-resourced public schools through co-location, construction, and other questionable contracts (Goodman, 2010). These are just a few examples of the ways in which political economic forces are decimating public education and each of these has very real consequences for students in American schools. These policies exponentially increase the inequity of an already unjust school system and demand the need for social justice activism to combat them.

Teachers who truly care about their students' opportunities and futures must play a role in the struggle against this wave of privatization and neoliberalism. Most teachers go into the profession because they "love children" and profess that they "want to make a difference" in their students' lives. I believe many teachers *do* want to do what's best for their students. What teachers are not told in their teacher education programs or in professional development workshops is that, to truly "make a difference" and to really do what's "best" for your students, you must work for justice both inside and outside of your classroom (New York Collective of Radical Educators, 2003). While it is overwhelming to think about "changing the world," it is reasonable to question whether, as a teacher, you are doing everything in your power to foster your students' educational and socio-emotional development. As demonstrated throughout this book, to only remain inside the classroom concerning yourself with mandated curriculum and high-stakes testing is to leave unaddressed the barriers that your students face on a daily basis. To fulfill your desire to be the best teacher possible, you must teach for justice in the classroom and organize for it in the streets.

NOTES

Chapter 2

1 Readings included authors such as Delpit, Hilliard, Howard, Kozol, Daniels-Tatum, Nieto, Chang & Au, and Ladson-Billings.

Chapter 3

1 Less than half of the cohort of 40 went into teaching the following year as many went directly to graduate school. Of those that did become teachers immediately, many returned to their hometowns to teach, significantly reducing the number of eligible participants.
2 The Jena Six refers to a racially charged situation that occurred in Jena, Louisana, in 2006 that gained national exposure in 2007. For more information, see www.democracy now.org/2007/7/10/the_case_of_the_jena_six.
3 Nick, a second-year teacher at the school, was an unusual ally for any CIPer. Also a former student of mine, Nick was equally committed to teaching issues of social justice.
4 New teachers are more likely to leave the profession than their seasoned counterparts: 14 percent of new teachers leave by the end of their first year, 33 percent leave within three years, and almost 50 percent leave in five years (Alliance for Excellent Education, 2004).

Chapter 4

1 Chantale had been a graduate student of mine at the same university. She was also a former student of mine, received similar pre-service education, and taught at the same school with three other participants.
2 As the facilitator/researcher of the group, I also received accolades for the group's success: from having related articles published in top journals to consulting jobs to invitations to present on our work.
3 Reina's participation in activities in support of Israel was difficult and complicated for me as someone who has a different stance on Israel/Palestine. Despite the fact that I did

not agree with her stance, I still must recognize her development as "successful" in terms of activism. She learned to research issues important to her and she moved from complacency to action.

Chapter 6

1 This quote came from Ella's analysis of an excellent article on teaching abolitionism by Bill Bigelow in Rethinking Schools, www.rethinkingschools.org/archive/25_02/25_02_bigelow.shtml.

BIBLIOGRAPHY

Acosta, Arce, Brummer, Carrion, Escamilla, Gonzalez, Gonzalez, Lopez, Martinez, & Sotelo v. Horne, Balantine, Moore, Haeger, Molera, Hamilton, Klein, Miller, Horton, Ortiz-Parsons, & Tyree (2010). '2010 SBA No. 7763' (October 18, 2010).

Agarwal, R., Epstein, S., Oppenheim, R., Oyler, C., & Sonu, D. (2010). 'From ideal to practice and back again: Beginning teachers teaching for social justice'. *Journal of Teacher Education*, 61(3), 237–47. doi:10.1177/0022487109354521.

Alexie, S. (2007). *The absolutely true diary of a part-time Indian*. New York, NY: Little, Brown Books for Young Readers.

Alliance for Excellent Education (2004). *Tapping the potential: Retaining and developing high-quality new teachers*. Washington, DC: Alliance for Excellent Education.

Anyon, J. (2005). *Radical possibilities: Public policy, urban education, and a new social movement*. New York, NY: Routledge.

——(1981). 'Social class and school knowledge'. *Curriculum Inquiry*, 11(1), 3–40.

Arce, S. (2010a). *TUSD Mexican American studies department: Presentation to the TUSD governing board* [PDF document]. Retrieved from http://ftpcontent.worldnow.com/kgun/KGUN/05%2013%20MASD%20Presentation.pdf.

Arce, S. (2010b, December 29). 'About us'. Retrieved from www.tusd.k12.az.us/contents/depart/mexicanam/about.asp.

Au, W., Bigelow, B., Burant, T., & Dawson, K. (Winter 2005/2006). 'Action education: Teacher organizers take quality into their own hands'. *Rethinking Schools*, 20(2). Retrieved from www.rethinkingschools.org/archive/20_02/orga202.shtml.

Aud, S., Hussar, W., Planty, M., Snyder, T., Bianco, K., Fox, M., & Drake, L. (2010). *The condition of education 2010 (NCES 2010–028)*. Washington, DC: National Center for Education Statistics, Institute of Education Sciences, US Department of Education.

Ayers, R. (2008). 'Classrooms, pedagogy, and practicing justice'. In Ayers, W. C., Quinn, T., & Stovall, D. (Eds.), *Handbook of social justice in education* (pp. 657–60). New York, NY: Routledge.

Ayers, W., Dohrn, B., & Ayers, R. (2001). *Zero tolerance: Resisting the drive for punishment in our schools: A handbook for parents, students, educators, and citizens*. New York, NY: New Press.

Ayers, W., Hunt, J. A., & Quinn, T. (1998). *Teaching for social justice: A democracy and education reader*. New York, NY: Teachers College Press.

Ayers, W. C., Quinn, T., & Stovall, D. (Eds.) (2008). *Handbook of social justice in education.* New York, NY: Routledge.

Bauer, S. & Richmond, T. (2011, February 17). 'Thousands protest Wisconsin anti-union bill'. *The Associated Press.* Retrieved from www.msnbc.msn.com/id/41624142/ns/politics-more_politics/t/thousands-protest-wisconsin-anti-union-bill/

Bell, P. (2004). 'On the theoretical breadth of design-based research in education'. *Educational Psychologist,* 39(4), 243–53. doi:10.1207/s15326985ep3904_6

Bergquist, L. & Stein, J. (2010, December 7). 'Walker looks at showdown with state employee unions: Governor-elect may try to guy bargaining power'. *JSOnline.* Retrieved from www.jsonline.com/news/statepolitics/111463779.html.

Bigelow, B., Christensen, L., Karp, S., Miner, B., & Peterson, B. (1994). 'Introduction: Creating classrooms for equity and social justice'. In Bigelow, B., Christensen, L., Karp, S., Miner, B., & Peterson, B. (Eds.), *Rethinking our classrooms: Teaching for equity and justice* (pp. 1–4). Milwaukee, WI: Rethinking Schools.

Biggers, J. (2011, November 17). 'Mexican American studies in Arizona needs no defense: It needs more defenders'. Retrieved from www.huffingtonpost.com/jeff-biggers/arizona-mexican-american-studies_b_1100131.html.

Bogdan, R. & Biklan, S. K. (1992). *Qualitative research for education: An introduction to theory and methods* (2nd ed.). Boston, MA: Allyn and Bacon.

Bowles, S. & Gintis, H. (1976). *Schooling in capitalist America: Educational reform and the contradictions of economic life.* New York, NY: Basic Books.

Bunting, E. (1991). *Fly away home.* New York, NY: Clarion Books.

Bush, S. (2011, May 17). 'Ethnic studies in Arizona'. *TucsonCitizen.com.* Retrieved from http://tucsoncitizen.com/three-sonorans/2011/05/17/ethnic-studies-in-arizona-former-mas-student-speaks-out/.

Camangian, P. (2010). 'Starting with self: Teaching autoethnography to foster critically caring literacies'. *Research in the Teaching of English,* 45(2), 179–204.

——(2008). 'Real talk: Transformative English teaching and urban youth'. In Ayers, W. C., Quinn, T., & Stovall, D. (Eds.), *Handbook of social justice in education* (pp. 497–507). New York, NY: Routledge.

Cammarota, J. & Romero, A. F. (2008). 'The social justice education project: A critically compassionate intellectualism for Chicana/o students'. In Ayers, W. C., Quinn, T., & Stovall, D. (Eds.), *Handbook of social justice in education* (pp. 465–76). New York, NY: Routledge.

Carlson, D. (1987). 'Teachers as political actors: From reproductive theory to the crisis of schooling'. *Harvard Educational Review,* 57(3), 283–308.

Cerecer, P. D., Gutiérrez, L. A., & Rios, F. (2010). 'Critical multiculturalism: Transformative educational principles and practices'. In Chapman, T. K. & Hobbel, N. (Eds.), *Social justice pedagogy across the curriculum: The practice of freedom* (pp. 144–63). New York, NY: Routledge.

Chang, B. & Au, W. (Winter 2007–8). 'You're Asian, how could you fail math?' *Rethinking Schools,* 22(2). Retrieved from www.rethinkingschools.org/archive/22_02/math222.shtml.

Chapman, T. K. & Hobbel, N. (Eds.) (2010). *Social justice pedagogy across the curriculum: The practice of freedom.* New York, NY: Routledge.

Christensen, L. (2009). *Teaching for joy and justice.* Milwaukee, WI: Rethinking Schools.

Chubbuck, S. M. (2010). 'Individual and structural orientations in socially just teaching: Conceptualization, implementation, and collaborative effort'. *Journal of Teacher Education,* 61(3), 197–210. doi:10.1177/0022487109359777.

Cochran-Smith, M. (2004). *Walking the road: Race, diversity, and social justice in teacher education.* New York, NY: Teachers College Press.

Cochran-Smith, M., Shakman, K., Jong, C., Terrell, D., Barnatt, J., & Mcquillan, P. (2009). 'Good and just teaching: The case for social justice in teacher education'. *American Journal of Education,* 115(3), 347–77.

Cooper, A. (Interviewer), Horne, T. (Interviewee), & Dyson, M. E. (2010). *Arizona Culture Clash* [Interview transcript]. Retrieved from http://transcripts.cnn.com/TRANSCRIPTS/1005/12/acd.01.html.

Counts, G. (1932). *Dare the school build a new social order?* New York, NY: Derek Day.

Delpit, L. (1992). 'Education in a multicultural society: Our future's greatest challenge'. *The Journal of Negro Education*, 61(3), 237–49.

Denham, D. (2008). *Teaching rebellion: Stories from the grassroots mobilization in Oaxaca.* Oakland, CA: PM Press.

Derman-Sparks, L. & Phillips, C. B. (1997). *Teaching/learning anti-racism: A developmental approach.* New York, NY: Teachers College Press.

Dewey, J. (1932). *The school and society.* Chicago, IL: University of Chicago Press.

Dixson, A. D. & Smith, J. D. (2010). 'Jump at da sun: Black feminist influences on social justice pedagogy'. In Chapman, T. K. & Hobbel, N. (Eds.), *Social justice pedagogy across the curriculum: The practice of freedom* (pp. 104–20). New York, NY: Routledge.

Doster, A. (2008, February 25). 'The Conscious Classroom'. *The Nation.*

Douglass, F. (1857). 'The significance of emancipation in the West Indies'. *The Frederick Douglass Papers.* Retrieved from http://memory.loc.gov/ammem/doughtml/doughome.html.

Duarte, A. (Winter 2009). 'TUSD MASD Alumni Profile: Adrian Laurenzi'. *Tezcatlipoca "Reflexiones", 2*(2). Retrieved from www.tusd.k12.az.us/contents/depart/mexicanam/newsletters.asp.

Duncan-Andrade, J. (2007). 'Gangstas, wankstas, and ridas: Defining, developing, and supporting effective teachers in urban schools'. *International Journal of Qualitative Studies in Education*, 20(6), 617–38.

Duncan-Andrade, J. M. R. (2005). 'Developing social justice educators'. *Educational Leadership*, 62(6), 70–73.

Duncan-Andrade, J. M. R. & Morrell, E. (2008). *The art of critical pedagogy: Possibilities for moving from theory to practice in urban schools.* New York, NY: Peter Lang.

Ely, M., Vinz, R., Anzul, M., & Downing, M. (1997). *On writing up qualitative research: Living by words.* London: Falmer Press.

Epstein, B. (Producer). (2010, March 10). *NBC Nightly News* [Television broadcast]. New York, NY: National Broadcasting Company.

FairTest. (2007, December 17). 'Dangerous consequences of high-stakes standardized testing'. Retrieved from http://fairtest.org/dangerous-consequences-highstakes-standardized-tes.

Fine, M. (2003). 'Invited testimony at Regents Hearing Standards and High School Graduation Requirements'. Albany, NY.

FoxNews.com. (2011, February 19). '"Fake" sick notes given to Wisconsin protesters amid anti-union bill faceoff'. Politics: State & Local. Retrieved from www.foxnews.com/politics/2011/02/19/saturdays-protests-wisconsin-expected-biggest/.

Freire, P. (1998). *Teachers as cultural workers: Letters for those who dare to teach.* Boulder, CO: Westview Press.

——(1970). *Pedagogy of the oppressed.* New York, NY: Herder & Herder.

Fuoco, M. (Producer) & Fedestin, B., Jean, J., Phillips, M., & Posada, M. (Creators). (2004). *The problem we all live with* [Motion picture]. (Available from What Kids Can Do, Inc., P.O. Box 603252, Providence, RI 02906)

Gabriel, T. & Medina, J. (2010, May 9). 'Charter schools' new cheerleaders: Financiers'. *New York Times.* Retrieved from www.nytimes.com/2010/05/10/nyregion/10charter.html.

Giroux, H. A. (1988). *Teachers as intellectuals: Toward a critical pedagogy of learning.* Westport, CT: Bergin & Garvey.

Goodman, A. (Interviewer), Gonzalez, J. (Interviewee). (2010). *Big banks making a bundle on new construction as schools bear cost.* Retrieved from Democracy now! The war and peace report website: www.democracynow.org/2010/5/7/juan_gonzalez_big_banks_making_a.

Goodreads (n.d.). 'Staceyann Chin > Quotable Quote'. Retrieved from www.goodreads. com/quotes/show/111119.

Greene, M. (1988). *The dialectic of freedom*. New York, NY: Teachers College Press.

Hackman, H. (2005). 'Five essential components for social justice education'. *Equity & Excellence in Education*, 38(2), 103–9.

Haimson, L. (2003). 'Invited testimony at Regents Hearing Standards and High School Graduation Requirements'. Albany, NY.

Harvard Graduate School of Education. (2010). *New national study finds increasing school segregation*. Retrieved from www.gse.harvard.edu/news_events/features/1999/orfieldde seg06081999.html.

Hayden, J. (Producer) & Hayden, J. (Director). (1996). *Children in America's schools with Bill Moyers* [Motion picture]. United States: South Carolina ETV.

Hilliard, A. G., III (2004) 'No mystery: Closing the achievement gap between Africans and excellence'. In Perry, T., Steele, C., & Hilliard, A., III (Eds.), *Young, gifted, and Black: Promoting high achievement among African American students* (pp. 131–66). Boston, MA: Beacon Press.

hooks, b. (1994). *Teaching to transgress: Education as the practice of freedom*. New York, NY: Routledge.

House Bill 2281, H.B. 2281, 49th Legislature. (2010). *House Bill 2281, H.B. 2281, 49th Legislature* Retrieved from www.azleg.gov.

Howard, G. R. (1999). *We can't teach what we don't know: White teachers, multiracial schools*. New York, NY: Teachers College Press.

Hursh, D. (2007). 'Assessing No Child Left Behind and the rise of neoliberal education policies'. *American Educational Research Journal*, 44(3), 493–518.

Huttleston, D. (2011, February 13). 'Top 10 things you should know about Scott Walker's budget repair bill'. [Web log comment]. Retrieved from www.bargainingforbenefits. com/2011/02/13/top-10-bombshells-in-scott-walkers-budget-repair-bill/.

Institute for Policy Studies Programs on Inequality and the Common Good. (2010). '[Graphic illustration re-creating the gap that gave us the Great Depression September 1, 2010]'. *Plutocracy reborn*. Retrieved from www.businessinsider.com/plutoc racy-reborn.

Irvine, J. J. (2003). *Educating teachers for diversity: Seeing with a cultural eye*. New York, NY: Teachers College Press.

Kailin, J. (2002). *Antiracist education: From theory to practice*. Lanham, MD: Rowman & Littlefield Publishers.

——(1999). 'How White teachers perceive the problem of racism in their schools: A case study in "liberal" Lakeview'. *Teachers College Record*, 100(4), 724–50.

Kapustka, K., Howell, P., Clayton, C., & Thomas, S. (2009). 'Social justice in teacher education: A qualitative content analysis of NCATE conceptual frameworks'. *Equity & Excellence in Education*, 42(4), 489–505.

Katsarou, E., Picower, B., & Stovall, D. (2010). 'Acts of Solidarity: Developing urban social justice educators in the struggle for quality public education'. *Teacher Education Quarterly*, 37(3), 137–154.

Kincheloe, J. L. (2005). *Critical pedagogy*. New York, NY: Peter Lang.

Kincheloe, J. L., & Steinberg, S. R. (1997). *Changing multiculturalism*. Buckingham: Open University Press.

King, J. E. (2008). 'Critical and qualitative research in teacher education: A blues epistemology, a reason for knowing for cultural well-being'. In Cochran-Smith, M., Feiman-Nemser, S., McIntyre, J., & Demers, K. (Eds.), *Handbook of research on teacher education: Enduring questions in changing contexts* (pp. 1094–1136) Mahwah, NJ: Erlbaum.

King, M. L. (1963, April 16). 'Letter from a Birmingham jail'. Retrieved from www.africa. upenn.edu/Articles_Gen/Letter_Birmingham.html.

Kozol, J. (2007, August). 'The big enchilada'. *Harper's Magazine,* 7–9.

——(2005). *The shame of the nation: The restoration of apartheid schooling in America*. New York, NY: Crown.

KQED (Producer). (1999, March 23). *Making the grade* [Bay Window Series]. San Francisco, CA: KQED-TV.

Kumashiro, K. K. (2008). *The seduction of common sense: How the right has framed the debate on America's schools*. New York, NY: Teachers College Press.

——(2004). *Against common sense: Teaching and learning toward social justice*. New York, NY: Routledge Falmer.

Labaree, D. F. (2004). *The trouble with ed schools*. New Haven: Yale University Press.

Ladson-Billings, G. (2001). *Crossing over to Canaan: The journey of new teachers in diverse classrooms* (1st ed.). San Francisco, CA: Jossey-Bass Publishers.

——(1994). *The dreamkeepers: Successful teachers of African American children* (1st ed.). San Francisco, CA: Jossey-Bass Publishers.

LaGravenese, R. (Director). (2007, January 5). *Freedom writers* [Motion picture]. United States: Paramount Pictures.

Lawrence, S. M. (1998). 'Unveiling positions of privilege: A hands-on approach to understanding racism'. *Teaching of Psychology*, 25, 198–200.

Leistyna, P. (2008). 'Preparing for public life: Education, critical theory, and social justice'. In Ayers, W. C., Quinn, T., & Stovall, D. (Eds.), *Handbook of social justice in education* (pp. 51–58). New York, NY: Routledge.

Lipman, P. (2005). '"This is America" 2005: The political economy of education reform against the public interest'. In Ladson-Billings, G. & Tate, W. F. (Eds.), *Education research in the public interest: Social justice, action, and policy* (pp. 98–118). New York, NY: Teachers College Press.

——(2004). *High stakes education: Inequality, globalization, and urban school reform*. New York, NY: Routledge/Falmer.

Loewen, J. (1996). *Lies my teacher told me: Everything your American history textbook got wrong*. New York, NY: Touchstone.

Lussenhop, J. (2011, February 23). 'Inside the multimillion-dollar essay-scoring business: Behind the scenes of standardized testing'. *City Pages*. Retrieved from www.citypages.com/2011-02-23/news/inside-the-multimillion-dollar-essay-scoring-business/.

McDonald, M. (2007). 'The joint enterprise of social justice teacher education'. *Teachers College Record*, 109(8), 2047–81.

McDonald, M. & Zeichner, K. M. (2008). 'Social justice teacher education'. In Ayers, W. C., Quinn, T., & Stovall, D. (Eds.), *Handbook of social justice in education* (pp. 595–610). New York, NY: Routledge.

McIntosh, P. (1988). *White privilege: Unpacking the invisible knapsack* [PDF document]. Retrieved from www.nymbp.org.

McKissack, F. (2007, Fall). 'Action education: Learning from Jena'. *Rethinking Schools*, 22 (1). Retrieved from www.rethinkingschools.org/archive/22_01/jena221.shtml.

McLaren, P. (2003). *Life in schools: An introduction to critical pedagogy in the foundations of education* (4th ed.). Boston, MA: Allyn & Bacon.

Marshall, C. & Anderson, A. L. (Eds.) (2009). *Activist educators: Breaking past limits*. New York, NY: Routledge.

Martinez, E. & Garcia, A. (2000, February 26). 'Global economy 101: What is "neo-liberalism"?' Retrieved January 15, 2009, from www.globalexchange.org/campaigns/econ101/neoliberalDefined.html.

Miech, R. A. & Elder, G. H. (1996). 'The service ethic and teaching'. *Sociology of Education*, 69(3), 237–53.

Mikel, E. R. & Hiserman, S. (2000). 'Beyond the classroom: Progressive activist teachers and images of experience, meaning, purpose, and identity'. In Joseph, P. B. & Burnaford, G. E. (Eds.), *Images of schoolteachers in America* (pp. 115–31). New York, NY: Routledge.

Miner, B. (Winter 2004/2005). 'Keeping public schools public: Testing companies mine for gold'. *Rethinking Schools*, 19(2). Retrieved from www.rethinkingschools.org/archive/19_02/test192.shtml.

Montano, T., Lopez-Torres, L., DeLissovoy, N., Pacheco, M., & Stillman, J. (2002) 'Teachers as activists: Teacher development and alternate sites of learning'. *Equity & Excellence in Education*, 35(3), 265–75. doi: 10.1080/10665680290175275

Montopoli, B. (2009, November 6). '237 millionaires in congress'. *CBS News*. Retrieved from www.cbsnews.com/8301–503544_162-5553408-503544.html.

Morrell, E. (2007). *Critical literacy and urban youth: Pedagogies of access, dissent, and liberation.* New York, NY: Routledge.

Network of Teacher Activist Groups. (2009, November 28). 'Mission'. Retrieved from http://teacheractivistgroups.org/.

——(n.d.). 'Current TAG organizations'. Retrieved December 15, 2009, from http://teacheractivistgroups.org/.

New York Collective of Radical Educators [NYCoRE]. (2003). 'Points of unity'. Retrieved from www.nycore.org/nycore-info/points-of-unity.

Nieto, S. (1999). *The light in their eyes: Creating multicultural learning communities.* New York, NY: Teachers College Press.

Nieto, Sonia & Bode, Patty (2008). *Affirming diversity: The sociopolitical context of multicultural education* (5th ed.). New York, NY: Allyn & Bacon.

Noddings, N. (1992). *The challenge to care in schools: An alternative approach to education.* New York, NY: Teachers College Press.

NOLA.com. (2011, February 18). 'Wisconsin protesters buoyed by delay on anti-union bill'. *The Associated Press*. Retrieved from www.nola.com/politics/index.ssf/2011/02/wisconsin_protesters_buoyed_by.html.

North, C. (2008). 'What is all this talk about "social justice"? Mapping the terrain of education's latest catchphrase'. *Teachers College Record*, 110(6), 1182–206.

Norton, M. I. & Sommers, S. R. (2011). 'Whites see racism as a zero-sum game that they are now losing'. *Perspectives on Psychological Science*, 6(3), 215–18. doi: 10.1177/1745691611406922

Oakes, J. & Lipton, M. (2007). *Teaching to change the world* (3rd ed.). Boston, MA: McGraw-Hill Higher Education.

Oakes, J., Rogers, J., & Lipton, M. (2006). *Learning power: Organizing for education and justice.* New York, NY: Teachers College Press.

Payne, C. M. & Strickland, C. S. (2008). *Teach freedom: Education for liberation in the African American tradition.* New York, NY: Teachers College Press.

Perez Huber, L., Johnson, R., & Kohli, R. (2007) 'Naming racism: A conceptual look at racism in US schools'. *Chicana/o Latina/o Law Review*, 26, 183–206.

Picower, B (in press). 'Learning to teach and teaching to learn: Supporting the development of new social justice educators'. *Teacher Education Quarterly*.

——(2011). 'Resisting compliance: Learning to teach for social justice in a neoliberal context'. *Teachers College Record*, 113(5). Retrieved June 1, 2011, from www.tcrecord.org/Content.asp?ContentID=16090.

——(2007). 'Supporting new educators to teach for social justice: The critical inquiry model'. *Penn Perspectives on Urban Education.* 5(1), 1–22.

——(2007). 'The unexamined Whiteness of teaching: Will the cycle be unbroken?' (doctoral dissertation, New York University, 2007). *Dissertation. Abstracts International*, AAT 3247768.

Pitzi, M. J. (2010, May 1). 'Arizona bill targets ban on ethnic studies'. *The Arizona Republic.* Retrieved from www.azcentral.com/news/election/azelections/articles/2010/05/01/20100501arizona-bill-bans-ethnic-studies.html.

Privatization of Public Schools. (2008) [PowerPoint slides]. Retrieved August 15, 2008, from www.nea.org/privatization/index.html.

Rodriguez, L. J. (1994). *Always running: La vida loca: Gang days in L.A.* New York, NY: Touchstone.

Rotherham, A. J. (2011, March 3). 'When it comes to class size, smaller isn't always better'. *TIME Magazine*. Retrieved from www.time.com/time/nation/article/0,8599,2056571,00.html.

Sandoval, W.A. & Bell, P. (2004). 'Design-based research methods for studying learning in context: Introduction'. *Educational Psychologist*, 39(4), 199–201.

Schey, R. & Uppstrom, A. (2009). 'Activist work as entry-year teachers: What we've learned'. In Blackburn, M. V., Clark, C. T., Kenney, L. M., & Smith, J. (Eds.), *Acting out! Combating homophobia through teacher activism* (pp. 88–102). New York, NY: Teachers College Press.

Schultz, B. D. (2008). *Spectacular things happen along the way: Lessons from an urban classroom*. New York, NY: Teachers College Press.

Schweisguth, M. (n.d.). 'Fair trade chocolate activity book'. Retrieved August 15, 2008, from www.globalexchange.org/cocoa.

Sewell, A. (2011, February 26). 'Protestors out in force nationwide to oppose Wisconsin's anti-union bill'. *Los Angeles Times*. Retrieved from http://articles.latimes.com/2011/feb/26/nation/la-na-wisconsin-protests-20110227.

Sleeter, C. E. (2007). *Facing accountability in education: Democracy and equity at risk*. New York, NY: Teachers College Press.

——(2005). *Un-standardizing curriculum: Multicultural teaching in the standards-based classroom*. New York, NY: Teachers College Press.

——(2001) 'Diversity vs. White privilege'. *Rethinking Schools*, 15(2).

Spalding, E., Klecka, C., Lin, E., Odell, S., & Jian, W. (2010). 'Social justice and teacher education: A hammer, a bell, and a song'. *Journal of Teacher Education*, 61(3), 191–96. doi:10.1177/0022487109359762.

Spring, J. (2009). *Deculturalization and the struggle for equality: A brief history of the education of dominated cultures in the United States* (6th ed.). New York, NY: McGraw-Hill Humanities/Social Sciences/Languages.

Stein, J., & Marley, P. (2011, February 10). 'Walker budget plan would limit state unions to negotiating only on salaries'. *JS Online*. Retrieved from www.jsonline.com/news/statepolitics/115726754.html.

Stern, S. (2006). 'The ed schools' latest—and worst—humbug'. *The City Journal*, 16(4), 42–63.

Tabb, W. (2001). 'Globalization and education as a commodity'. *Clarion Summer 2001*. Retrieved January 15, 2009, from www.psc-cuny.org/jcglobalization.htm.

Tan, L. (2008). *The 5 E's of emancipatory pedagogy: The rehumanizing approach to teaching and learning with inner city youth*. In Ayers, W. C., Quinn, T., & Stovall, D. (Eds.), *Handbook of social justice in education* (pp. 485–96). New York, NY: Routledge.

Tatum, B. D. (1999). *"Why are all the Black kids sitting together in the cafeteria?" and other conversations about race*. New York, NY: Basic Books.

ThinkExist.com Quotations. (2011, May 1). *Margaret Mead quotes*. Retrieved from http://thinkexist.com/quotes/Margaret_Mead/.

Tillage, W. (1997). *Leon's story*. New York, NY: Farrar, Straus & Giroux.

Toch, T. (2006). *Margins of error: The education testing industry in the No Child Left Behind era* [PDF document]. Retrieved from www.educationsector.org/usr_doc/Margins_of_Error.pdf.

Traub, J. (2003, August 3). 'New York's new approach'. *New York Times*. Retrieved from www.nrrf.org/article_traub_8-3-03.htm.

US Department of Education, National Center for Education Statistics, Schools and Staffing Survey (SASS). (2008). *Public school teacher and private school teacher data files*. Retrieved from http://nces.ed.gov/programs/coe/tables/table-tsp-1.asp.

US Social Forum. (2010). *General format*. Retrieved from www.ussf2010.org/.

Valenzuela, A. (1999). *Subtractive schooling: US-Mexican youth and the politics of caring*. New York, NY: SUNY Press.

Villegas, A. M. (2008, March). 'Diversifying the workforce: Examining induction, retention, and development of new teachers of color'. Paper presented at American Educational Research Association Conference, New York, NY.

Weiner, L. (2006). 'Challenging deficit thinking'. *Educational Leadership*, 64(1), 42–45.

Westheimer, J. & Kahne, J. (2007). 'Service learning and democracy: Responding to the issues'. *Equity & Excellence in Education*, 40(2), 97–100.

Westheimer, J. & Suurtamm, K. E. (2008). *The politics of social justice meets practice: Teacher education and school change*. In Ayers, W. C., Quinn, T., & Stovall, D. (Eds.), *Handbook of social justice in education* (pp. 589–94). New York, NY: Routledge.

Zeichner, K. (1993). 'Connecting genuine teacher development to the struggle for social justice'. *Journal of Education for Teaching*, 19(1), 5–20.

Zinn, H. (2003). *A people's history of the United States: 1492–present*. New York, NY: Harper Perennial.

——(2002). *You can't be neutral on a moving train: A personal history of our times*. Boston, MA: Beacon Press.

INDEX

Page numbers in *italics* denotes a diagram/table

Prescott Elementary School 15
privatization 1, 2, 69, 115
Problem We All Live with, The
    (documentary) 43
public, going 55, 66–7, 68

questioning, critical 92

racism 3, 11; deflection of personal
    responsibility towards dealing with 24,
    24, 37–9, 48–50; denial of existence
    of 23, *24*, 25–9, *25*, 42–5; historical
    27–8, 29, 31, 41, 60; missionary
    approach 24, *24*, 39–41, 50–2;
    oppositional stances towards 23–41,
    112; recognizing of as prerequisite to
    teaching for social justice 13; refuting
    of role in by teachers 24, *24*, 29–33,
    45–7
responsibility, deflection of personal 24,
    24, 37–9, 48–50
reverse racism 22
rich: gap between poor and 114

safe haven, building a 55, 61–3, 68
schools-to-prison pipeline 2, 115
Secret, C. 15
slavery 27, 28, 29–30; abolition of 113–14
social action: as curriculum,13; as moving
    beyond curriculum 9, 68, ; with
    students 12, 90–95, challenges to
    taking, 71, 72, 74–77, 79, 80, 81–82,
social change: and understanding of by
    teacher activists 9, 12, 82, 84, 85
Social Justice Critical Inquiry Project *see* CIP
social justice education/educators (SJE):
    content mastery as key component of
    6; definition and meaning of 3–4, 5;
    and democratic classrooms 6;
    oppressive policies fought 9; outside
    the classroom 5, 7, 8–10, 12; and
    student-teacher relationship 5–6;
    teaching root causes of inequality
    6–7; within the classroom 5–7, 11
social justice education (SJE) strategies
    54–70; awareness of existence of
    broader movement of SJE 62;
    building a safe haven 55, 61–3, 68;
    camouflaging critical pedagogy 55,
    63–4, 68; developing students as
    activists 64–6, 68; going public 55,
    66–7, 68; and historical content
    knowledge 58; preparing and

supporting students to change the
    world 55, 90–108; resisting of
    mandated curriculum 57; teaching in
    a state of fear 56–61
Spring, J.: *Deculturalization and the Struggle
    for Equality* 44
standardized testing 57, 58–9
students: developing as activists by teachers
    64–6, 68; lack of faith in by teachers
    to participate in social action 81–2;
    lack of historical knowledge 7, 44,
    58; preparing and supporting of to
    change the world 90–5, 108–9;
    relationship with teachers 5–6, 93, 95
substitution, tools of *see* tools of inaction

TAG (Teacher Activist Groups) 1–2, 87
talk show activity 47–8
Teacher Action Group in Philadelphia 1
Teacher Activist Groups (TAG) 1–2, 10,
    87, 110,
teacher activism/activists 1–16, 87–111;
    barriers to 10–11; challenges to
    moving outside of the classroom 12;
    and collective organizing 8–10, 96–7;
    creating curriculum around cultural
    diversity of their classes 93;
    engagement in action in several ways
    8; getting their voices into the policy
    arena 97–8; issues involved with 2, 9;
    levels engaged on 17; moving toward
    liberation commitment 88, 90–108;
    organizations created 1–2; preparing
    and supporting students to change
    the world 55, 90–5, 108–9; reasons
    for persistence of 113–14; reconciling
    the vision commitment 87–8, 88–90;
    see students as directors of learning
    93; standing up to oppression
    commitment 88, 95–9; supporting of
    students' personal development 94–5;
    and teacher education 3, 52, 53, 60,
    62, 110; understanding about social
    change 9, 12, 82, 84, 85; working on
    issues of educational justice 9
teacher attrition 69
teacher education 7, 53; and social
    justice/teacher activism 3, 52, 53,
    60, 62, 110
teacher lay-offs 1, 2, 77, 100, 108, 113,
teachers: balancing work with personal life
    83; depiction of by politicians 1;
    disconnection between life